THE CONTEMPLATION
OF THE WORLD

THE CONTEMPLATION OF THE WORLD

Figures of Community Style

Michel Maffesoli

Translated by Susan Emanuel

 University of Minnesota Press
Minneapolis
London

The University of Minnesota Press gratefully acknowledges financial
assistance provided for the translation of this book by the French
Ministry of Culture.

Originally published as *La contemplation du monde: Figures du style
communautaire*. Copyright 1993 Éditions Grasset & Fasquelle, Paris.

Published by the University of Minnesota Press
111 Third Avenue South, Suite 290, Minneapolis, MN 55401-2520
Printed in the United States of America on acid-free paper

Library of Congress Cataloging-in-Publication Data

Maffesoli, Michel.
    [Contemplation du monde. English]
    The contemplation of the world : figures of community style /
Michel Maffesoli ; translated by Susan Emanuel.
      p.   cm.
    Includes index.
    ISBN 0-8166-2688-X (hc)
    ISBN 0-8166-2689-8 (pb)
    1. Aesthetics. 2. Postmodernism.   I. Title.
BH39.M3213   1996
194—dc20   95-41472

194
m187

CONTENTS

PREFACE

... it is a poem, the last poem in a world where the frozen
blood of the damned is mixed with the ardent faith of
those who have never had anything to lose, the comba-
tants of the futile, of the almost nothing, of nothingness.
    YVES SIMON, *La Dérive des Sentiments*

The Communitarian Debate

DREAM AND THOUGHT ARE CLOSELY linked, especially
during times in which societies dream themselves. Therefore
it is important to know how to accompany these dreams, all
the more so when their denial is, generally speaking, a constant of all dictatorships. The latter no longer wear the brutal
mask they had throughout modernity. They assume the pleas-
ing aspect, somewhat sanitized, of happiness at a cut-rate
price. Modern *dictatorship,* apart from notable exceptions, is
not even a case of bloodthirsty and cruel individuals; rather it
is anonymous, gentle, and sly. It is above all unconscious of
what it is, or what it does, and occupies itself, in completely
good faith, in promoting the sacrosanct principle of utilitarian reality. And it thereby extirpates, in effect, the oneiric fac-
ulty, the ability to dream. In this sense it merely expresses a

constant in human history: the powers-that-be rest easy when no one can, or knows how to, or dares any longer to, dream.

In pursuing the *debate* with social life, that is, in continuing to be attentive to the *customs and uses* of basic sociality, I would like to stress the subtle link existing between concern for the present, daily life, and the imaginary—in a word, the aesthetic, here understood in its widest meaning: that of empathy, of *communitarian* desire, of shared emotion or vibration. In this respect, one could cite Bakunin, the eternal troublemaker, and along with him stress that "in all of history there is a quarter reality, at least three quarters imagination and . . . throughout history it is by no means this imaginary part that has acted the least powerfully on men."[1] This is a judicious remark if there ever was one, which well demonstrates that beyond (or short of) political activism there exists a form of *sensitive quietism* that is not a minor factor in socialization. It is an ethic of the aesthetic, so to speak.

After more than two centuries of economic and and political domination, it is now necessary to know how to swim against the current, with the risks that it involves, in order to explore the vast domain of the collective imaginary that, for lack of being thought through, is largely lived within daily life. This collective imaginary has nothing to do with what might be a new form of irrationalism, or a manifestation of a renascent obscurantism, but it delimits the sphere of the nonrational or of the nonlogical, whose social import can no longer be denied. It is in this sense that thinking is a work of endurance, of exigency requiring an effort, and calling for a true initiation.

Such an initiation may be a form of elitism, if one understands by that the concern to make the reader participate in the dynamic of thought. It is not a question of "producing" or unveiling a truth that is already there, or even of giving ready-made answers to all the problems permeating our mutating societies. Their urgency, it is true, gives rise to impatience. Here is another reason to temporize, to establish comparisons, to raise questions—in short, to learn to pose problems more than to offer their solutions.

There is a practice belonging to medieval monasticism, that of the *lectio divina,* which may in this respect be useful to us. In ruminating on the word of God, and the diverse texts that comment on it, the monk penetrated himself into them, and thus penetrated their profound meaning. Perhaps the same is true of the text of the social realm. In tackling it from many sides, and in ruminating on both its dead ends and its dazzling explosions of insight, one may participate in the collective experience and in the mystery of which it is the expression. It is, in any case, such an initiatory step that I am offering the reader.

It is from such a perspective, bowing to some great ancestors—Sigmund Freud, Max Weber, Walter Benjamin—that one may give the essay form its title of nobility, that of true intellectual status. The sociological essay, in particular, is thus the closest to its object, and the closest to social life, meaning merely a series of "essays" or infinite attempts that is never concluded. In this sense, just like the novel or the poem, the essay is just re-creation starting from the elements constitutive of that life. Thus—and this is the dynamic aspect of a work in progress—one may be content to enter into an uninterrupted conversation with one's century.

This chat is conducted by each writer starting from a few obsessive ideas, which may be compared to musical variations on a known theme; embroidery around a melody of which the writer is not the master: the melody of social rhythm. The latter is totally autonomous. And the author must be content, starting precisely from those haunting ideas, to bring forth a few strong beats, to accentuate one aspect or another, to offer some accompaniment or other—all of which have as a sole objective to make us aware of the originality of that very rhythm at a given moment. Just as there is no *philosophia perennnis,* so the social field is always dependent on its epoch. This results in a contrapuntal writing made up of perpetual variations, around an object that is never explicable in its totality, and whose sole ambition is to grasp its essential characteristics, to discern its contours, and to show its consequences in the here and now.[2] One finds here the approach proposed by Edmond Jabès, for whom, alongside a Cartesian thought developing such a fine mechanics of demonstrations founded on the principle of causality, there exists another manner of doing things, one that proceeds, like the sea by the shore, by successive waves.

I will say and do the same thing in this book. Paralleling an elusive object in constant mutation, one must apply a labile and sinuous kind of thinking process, one that does not fear repetitions. Each of these repetitions in fact brings its specific touch, thus allowing the perfection or the completion of the picture embarked upon. The impressionism thereby induced is all the more necessary when the epoch is marked by heterogeneity and does not allow itself to be reduced to a concept or even to an ensemble of concepts. In classical scientific analysis, when confronted with a dead or stabilized object, one can shift, according to legitimately admissible requirements, from the concrete to the abstract. It is totally otherwise when a new culture, in its nascent state, is bubbling with effervescence. From here on, one must adopt an intellectual posture that, with suppleness, is content to describe, to take note, to "monstrate" that which is—even if, in many ways, this state of affairs is monstrous.

One may also refer to André Gide, whose work is constructed as the "burgeoning of a theme."[3] Thus all his analyses and all his fictions take shape from the burgeoning of a life that is more or less obscure, and they are engaged in achieving an understanding of each of the concrete branches that constitute it. Although less classical, this is also a work of intelligent understanding. It seems as if the somewhat dense and bushy baroque in which we are living incites us to such an approach, and, more than to general and abstract propositions, it invites us to bring our attention to bear on "the most extreme concrete" (Walter Benjamin), all of whose elements, as minuscule as they may be, interact so as to result in the complex society we know.

It is important to note that this complex society rests on an ensemble of values that did not have established rights within social life; at best they were confined to the private realm. Moreover, they were granted no academic dignity. This was the case for what relates to *communitarianism,* to the quotidian, to localism, to the present, the passionate, and of course the imaginary in all its different modulations. Here we are concerned with all those banalities, which it is useful to analyze at a time when, after the bankruptcy of the grand ideological causes, it is urgent to come back to the essential problems of a life without qualities.

Sine ira et odio

Thinking with detachment is, ultimately, a good guarantee against dogmatism, without thereby entailing an abdication of the intellect. Quite the contrary: in periods of turbulence, it is better to tackle social phenomena in a spirit free of all prejudice, or at the very least in a spirit exempt as much as possible from preconceived ideas. This is because it is truly a continual metamorphosis that is under way before our very eyes. I have already spoken of the "transfiguration" of the political.

But pushing the analysis further, one may observe that it is the whole of society that is affected by the usurious passing of time, whence comes a species of *palingenesis* that this induces. I mean to say that, by a sort of cyclical process, a total re-creation is carried out starting from chaos. More specifically, the saturation of the values of modernity tends to give way to alternative values with still ill-defined outlines, but whose efficacy no one can deny.

It is precisely to analyze better these renascent values that one must know how to break with intellectual orthodoxy, hence the acknowledgment of tribalism (in my earlier book *Le Temps des Tribus*) and of the aesthetisization of existence (in *Aux Creux des Apparences*). Here are values that one may, sometimes quite rightly, fight against, but whose increasing importance cannot be denied. They express, manifestly, a fatigue with regard to the political or rather toward the democratic ideal that developed slowly throughout modernity. To deny them is no longer possible, to disclaim them is not serious. Nor can one any longer be content with considering them as marginal; it is possible to condemn them morally, but that does not make them disappear. Moreover, many are those who, having ignored them, now use the very term *tribalism* or the thematic of the aesthetic. So it is urgent, from a purely speculative viewpoint (as is mine here) or from the perspective of action or reaction, to appreciate the social consequences of the emergence of these values.

To put it rather abruptly, one can ask oneself if the democratic ideal that was the mark of modernity is not being succeeded by a *communitarian ideal*,[4] which—like everything in a nascent state, or rather in a renascent one—is developing in pain and uncertainty. I do mean "renaissance," since to a large extent it gives meaning once more to the archaic elements that one would have believed totally crushed by the rationalization of the world. The diverse religious fanaticisms, the ethnic resurgences, the linguistic claims or other attachments to territories are the most evident manifestations of this archaism. But the same applies to all enthusiasms of whatever order they may be—sporting, musical, or festive, those effervescent demonstrations punctuating social life— without forgetting the fury of consumption that gives the great megalopolises the appearance of a perpetual bazaar where unprecedented conspicuous consumption is being celebrated. All this is expressed in a more or less paroxysmal manner, but in every case, there is something of the antique trance, which essentially had as its function to comfort the being-togetherness *(l'être ensemble)* of those who participated in the same mysteries.

The communitarian ideal is equally encountered in the multiple forms of solidarity and generosity that one too often neglects to analyze. They may be more or less spectacular; they may be channeled by the media or, on the contrary, be lived out on the quiet level of the quotidian. Nevertheless, they are no less important elements of basic sociability: the concerts for great humanitarian causes, the multiplication of "nongovernmental organizations" and the commitment they arouse, the various charitable initiatives, the recrudescence of "good works"—without forgetting the diverse idealisms that, without very much theory, are essentially addressed to the affective side of those who practice them. In all these instances, while the efficacy may not be evident—and it is even sometimes totally nil—nevertheless, in a more or less conscious manner, a form of being-togetherness is lived out that is no longer oriented to the faraway, toward the realization of a perfect society in the future, but rather is engaged in managing the present, which one tries to make as hedonistic as possible.

The sensibility that underpins all these manifestations, the paroxysmal as well as the mundane, has already been analyzed. I have even spoken in this respect of a *culture of sentiment*. It now remains to be seen what the cause is and what the effects of it may be. One cannot reduce this renascent culture to its conceptual or rational aspect, the latter being, moreover, impoverished as well as translated, most of the time, into an ideological bric-a-brac that does not merit great attention. Thus one can see an ensemble of images at work that, by successive additions, manage to constitute a collective consciousness serving as underpinning both to the whole of social life and to diverse "tribes" that take part in it. In this respect, in opposition to those who continue to analyze the contemporary world with the categories specific to modernity, one could speak of the reenchantment of the world. It is, in fact, this which is at issue and which may allow us to grasp the mysterious vision of things at work in the communitarianism in question here. The mystery is precisely what one person shares with some others, and that consequently serves as cement, flatters the sentiment of belonging, and so favors a new relation with the social environment and with the natural environment.

There exist numerous ways of approaching this communitarian ideal. In this book I will propose some that can be summarized by two key words: *style* and *image*. The chapters, shaped on the basis of these terms, are not enclosed within themselves, but, on the contrary, respond to, complement, as well as nuance each other. The examples that I use—taken from theoretical works, whether philosophical, sociological, or historical, or even taken, quite simply, from empirical reality—can recur in each chapter. The whole is to be understood as delimiting the "imagistic" world that is being sketched before us; by this I mean a complex ensemble in which the diverse manifestation of the image, of the imaginary, of the symbolic, and the play of appearances occupy a preeminent place in all domains.

To style first. It is not a matter of understanding it in its narrow sense, but rather as the general frame in which social life is expressed at a given moment. Thus, just as one could speak of a theological style in the Middle Ages or of an economic style in modernity (and certainly up until the most recent decades), I will try to show that an aesthetic style is in the course of being elaborated in front of us. In this sense, nearest to its etymological meaning, "style" is that by which an epoch defines itself, writes itself, and describes itself.

Once this framework has been set up, I will analyze the significance of the profusion of images to which it gives birth. The image, let us not forget, was always suspect in Western tradition. It was the "madwoman of the hearth" *(la folle du logis),* capable of the worst perversions. By a curious transmutation of values, this image now becomes a "link": it unites us to the surrounding world, it unites me to others who surround me. One could illustrate this with one of its modulations: the object. Moving beyond stigmatization or moralistic condemnation, I will try to show that the object does not isolate, but that it is, on the contrary, a vector of communion. Like the totem for primitive tribes, it serves as a pole of attraction for postmodern tribes. In this sense the image and what I call the "imaged object" are opposed to rationalism and to the distant ideal that prevailed throughout modernity.

These are the key ideas that will guide us through the initiatory steps I spoke of. They do not lead to a definite conclusion. Could there be such a conclusion, since essentially it is a matter of describing a dynamic in full flow? Reading these lines, one is not going to find prepackaged answers. It suffices for the time being to make an inventory of the hieroglyphs by which a society speaks and lives itself. But such an inventory is by no means useless, since the hieroglyphs are certainly the signs of the sacred, of that by which a social ensemble holds together, what assures it of its roots and nourishes its being.

The reader will be aware that I am contradicting a number of conventional ideas and trying here to show that style and image no longer have anything to do with the individualism of modernity. The very principle of individualization, and the individual who is its expression, seem to me to be totally saturated, used up. The subject is no longer master of himself and already no longer masters the universe. The social, in its rational and mechanical form, which grew out of such a configuration, is therefore no longer on the agenda. But this is not to say that there does not exist an alternative being-togetherness. And while it may not be totally clear unto itself, such a thing is certainly present. Although it is not conscious, it is really lived as such. In a provisional manner, one could say that the imaginal world is both cause and effect of a "mass subjectivity" that progressively permeates all domains of social life. The latter no longer rests on triumphant reason, it no longer has anything to do with a contractual attitude, but rather is turned toward the future. But it can be discerned in emotionalism, in shared sentiment and common passion—all the Dionysiac values that relate to the here and now, the "hic et nunc," to worldly hedonism. This is just what gives rise to the play of images and their viral dissemination. In this unreal meaning, in the form of the diverse components I have just mentioned, lie the best means of understanding the real—that is, that which gives itself to be lived in the efflorescence of the daily tragedy.

I. TREATISE ON STYLE

We think that hidden in the creation of a new style is the
unique and sublime possibility of making life bearable.
 ERNST JÜNGER, *Gardens and Streets*

By Way of Introduction

THE TERM "GENIUS" DESERVES TO RECOVER its widest
meaning: for example, the genius of a place, or the genius of a
people. This broader interpretation is quite difficult after
more than three centuries of modernity in which an individualist ideology has prevailed. But if we are attached to thinking
in the present, to thinking *of* the present, and if we wish to understand the shifts in importance that are being detected today, it behooves us to give back to collective genius its titles of
nobility. It is at this price that the different aspects of social
life will find not a meaning (in that this term implies the univocal, intangible, and universal—as with progress, historical
evolutionism, or national and international legal arrange-
ments) but rather their varied significations: significations
that are lived alongside others and are the causes and effects
of a new way of being together.

This is really what is at issue: individualism, instrumental reason, the omnipotence of technique, and the "everything is economics" no longer arouse the adherence of former times, and they no longer function as founding myths or as goals to be attained. In other words, the democratic ideal is saturated and in the course of being replaced by what we could call the communitarian ideal. Therefore it is important to discern the outlines of the shape the latter will assume.

Let us be clear about this: to appeal to the notion of collective genius, of the will to live to which it gives impulse, is by no means some sort of nostalgia for a social order that has vanished. Nor is it a question of regretting some premodern community of indefinite shape, but rather of recognizing that this world coming to its conclusion is being succeeded by a new style of existence.[1] One thinks of the *corsi* and *ricorsi,* of the steps forward and backward that, according to Giambattista Vico, characterize human history. To put it yet another way, and if one does not envisage it within a mechanically dialectic perspective, one could refer to the effect of the negative: that which we might have believed to be outmoded, after having secretly bored into the body social, comes back to the forefront. Specifically, this means the return of images, the importance of emotional contagion, the recourse to those multiple symbolisms that are the affirmation of religious identification, ethnic effervescence, the search for "territory"—all things that serve as a matrix for a budding sociality, all things that constitute the cultural stew of which the headlines offer us countless examples of a more or less explosive nature.

No society escapes this gestating style. This is evident for the former empire of the "East." And it is the same for the turbulences that affect different countries of the so-called third world. But the Western countries—this "first world" of modernity—are themselves in a state of profound crisis. As for the "second world," the American empire, which seems to serve as a model or guarantee of a new world order, it is nothing but a colossus with feet of clay—it, too, is on the brink of implosion. All this is quite banal, but worth recalling not in a catastrophic or apocalyptic manner, but quite simply to make us attentive to these *ricorsi* of which Vico spoke: regularly, there are renewals or, one might say, reprovisioning from the stock of imaginal ideas and common myths, serving as the conditions of possibility of any life in society.

This is what makes us speak of a collective genius. There is something creative in the air, even if it has need, in order to be affirmed, of a destructive phase. To put it in a nutshell, what is anomic today will be canonic tomorrow. From this arises the need for concentrated attention to those collective dreams that sometimes express themselves in paroxysm and in fury, taking the form of fanaticism and exclusion, and that sometimes are lived in the most uninventive kind of corporatism, in daily drudgery, in juvenile revolt, or in sector-based demands that are all the more violent for being, most often, "nonrational." All these are throwbacks to primitive impulses, kinds of archaisms that could be compared to what Wilfred Pareto called "residues" and that govern, whether one wishes it or not, that instinct for aggregation, that mysterious "social attraction" (Patrick Tacussel) of which the social tissue is made.

Perhaps we ought to speak in this respect of the birth of a "collective ego," no longer recognized in ideals that are remote, rational, universal, suitable for the nation-states of modernity, but drawing its strength from the nearby, from daily living—what Benjamin called, gladly, "the most extreme concrete." There is in fact an obvious parallel to be made between the saturation of the political and the reactualization of the "domestic," of the ecological, which step by step infects the whole of the planet. Certainly such a process is by no means uniform, and it assumes numerous variations. But like a groundswell that nothing can halt, this movement is going to determine, in the end, the social configuration of the century to come.

Regarding the shock wave of the French Revolution, whose importance in the elaboration of the democratic ideal we know, Pierre-Simon Ballanche was able in the nineteenth century to speak of a veritable "palingenesis," of a total change. Perhaps it is the same thing today. A few decades ago a profound metamorphosis began that, in organic fashion, grafted itself onto preexisting germs. These germs have already been flagged: tribalization, a culture of sentiment, the aesthetisization of life, the dominance of the mundane. They are about to constitute a new configuration of the world that may be deplored or celebrated—that is beside the point—but that it is urgent to analyze. This configuration delineates, in its strictest sense, the style of the epoch: I mean to say that which orients or writes the epoch. Hence there is nothing frivolous about attention to style, defined in this way. On the contrary, it is what may make all the microevents stand out, all the imperceptible mutations, the apparently anecdotal situations that back-to-back make up culture; that is, they serve as substrate, compost, for that creation which is a whole social life.

Ballanche's palingenesis, the process of metamorphosis it implies, is a pertinent angle of attack for apprehending social phenomena. It allows us to give nuance to brutal ruptures, to epistemological breaks, and to other thematics of the "end" of mankind, of the social, of history—all of which are nourished by the various catastrophe theories of modern thought. In fact, in this respect akin to Leibniz, Ballanche stresses continuities, the imperceptible transitions or, to put it in more sociological terms, the power of the instituting and nascent state of things.² Common sense, in an unconscious manner, experiences and practices this incessant to-and-fro between one conviction and another; the versatility of public opinion is its ultimate expression. So do historians and sociologists who stress the "law of the blunting effect" *(loi de l'émoussement)* or the mechanism of saturation (Pitirim Sorokin). By this they underline the fact that when something has lost its attraction, we pass imperceptibly to another reference object onto which we bring to bear veneration or attraction. Fashion is a proof of this. Hence a new form of sensibility is being born.

The history of art is in this respect instructive, since it shows how change in style is cause and effect of change in sensibility. Ruskin indicated as much for the shift from the Romanesque to the Gothic, Wölfflin for that which goes from the Renaissance to the baroque, and one could at leisure multiply such examples. In each case—this is what concerns me here—style is the essential characteristic of a collective sentiment. It is its specific mark. In the strict meaning of the term, it becomes an all-encompassing form, a "forming form" that gives birth to whole manners of being, to customs, representations, and the various fashions by which life in society is expressed.

Quite evidently—and here I recall what I said about imperceptible transitions—the distinction among styles is not clearcut; one may assign them precise limits, but these are pure convention. In fact, there are contaminations, overlappings, or even, to borrow an expression from the philosopher Ernst Bloch, "noncontemporaneities." This is particularly the case in transitional periods, during which there continue to exist concurrently, in a more-or-less vibrant form, antinomian lifestyles, and when the institutional—the political, intellectual, administrative, religious "establishment"—endeavors to preclude as much as it can the expression of vibrant forces of the instituting, of the anomic.

To complicate matters further, we may recall that there are bizarre resurgences—a kind of historical déjà vu. Citing Oswald Spengler, Ernst Jünger reflects that "phenomena, personalities, events, even though separated by millennia, can be contemporaneous one with another."[3] This morphological point of view is interesting, in the sense that it relativizes the originality of a given civilization, and especially because it corrects the linear, evolutionary, and progressivist pretensions of the Western philosophy of history. In reality, both of these perspectives, the overlapping of styles (especially during periods of transition) and the cyclical return of the events and "types" of past history, are useful in helping us understand the specificity of the postmodern style that, in many aspects, rests on a syncretism, on a melange of genres, and on the multiform reutilization of elements of the "good old days." Folklore, the passion for genealogical research, the celebration of the soil and its products, architectural postmodernism, and the use made of mythology in video clips or advertising are, from this point of view, most illuminating.

The very property of a particular style is to be heterogeneous, even to rest on contradictory tendencies. We should remember the difficulty that early Christianity had in distinguishing itself from diverse pagan practices. For example, the difference between images of the Virgin Mary and those of Venus was not, for a long time, evident. The same was true of Catholic saints, who for the most part were merely heroes, gods, or great local personages who had been hastily baptized. And the "spirits" of Afro-Brazilian cults, or other forms of voodoo, essentially function on such a contamination of styles.

Once this nuance is discerned, we must nevertheless recognize that after a preliminary mixing, the interaction of styles leads to a global style that gives everything, according to M.

Shapiro's expression, an "identical tonality," with the style of an epoch becoming henceforth an "ensemble of characteristic forms."[4] This global unity merits attention. As I said earlier, it is a dynamic unity, fluid and supple, but it no less delineates the outlines of the cultural model of the given epoch.[5] The terms *pattern* in sociology, *épistémé* (Michel Foucault) in the history of ideas, *paradigm* (Thomas Kuhn) in the history of science, or even the "semantic basin" such as utilized by Gilbert Durand in anthropology all designate the same thing: one can in a holistic manner gather together the different elements that make up society, show their interactions, and detect the common thread that unites them.

Some Generalities on Style

It is often considered that "style makes the man," and this conventional thought serves, in principle, to relegate style to the private sphere. In this sense, it is a surplus, a supplement of the soul reserved for literature or for other great works of culture such as painting, music, and sculpture. In all these cases, it concerns only leisure, life's Sundays, without too many implications for the rest of existence, which is subject to a reality principle that is definitely more serious. In this perspective, style, like the dancer the bourgeois "bought himself" for his relaxation, is revocable at will, particularly in times of crisis. Certainly there has been over the past few years another use of the notion, especially in the expression "lifestyle," but it was essentially employed to a mercantile end, since it was a question of discerning "targeted" groups with a view to adjusting production and consumption to their demands and their desires, supposed or real.

Without denying the importance of style in "great" culture, and without neglecting its metaphoric use for market studies,

it is suitable to give it a much wider acceptation, which would
be of a measure with the social stakes it represents. Already at
the end of the nineteenth century, certain sociologists (such as
Jean-Marie Guyau) saw the problem clearly, in showing that
style was "the society of an epoch"—or more precisely, that
the style of any man, or of any given group, was merely the
crystallization of the epoch in which he or it lived. This gave
style another amplitude and above all allowed it to serve as
revelatory of social complexity. It follows that style will be
applied to art, but equally to sentiments, to social relations, to
industrial production, or to business life. Thus one sees how
this conception of a complex style is most pertinent for appreciating all nascent things, stressing what is apparently useless,
which runs from the aesthetisization of existence to enterprise
culture, and including industrial design and the care taken
over the quality of life that characterizes contemporary urbanism.

Style defined as "the society of an epoch" also recalls the notion of "climate" used by the history of ideas and which allows
us to understand how the values of a given epoch are born,
flourish, and finally bear fruit.[6] What is true of the production
of ideas can be extrapolated to social life in its entirety. Just as
one must grasp a particular philosophy or religion on the basis
of the social climate that gave rise to it, so it is possible to understand the present on the basis of this same climate that is—
and this is not merely a metaphor—the condition of possibility
for the emergence and the growth of any social life, which is
another way of saying the society of a given epoch.

Moreover, one can specify that, in a simple society (which
was the case for the modern epoch, when everything rested on
distinction, separation, breaks—for example, with the economic well separated from culture and the latter from religion), style could be something apart, which was applied to

the well-circumscribed domain of art. It is otherwise for complex societies, traditional societies, and certainly postmodern societies: since all domains of social life are in interaction, it is very difficult, if not impossible, to isolate one aspect or another of a phenomenon. In this case, style can be understood as the "principle of unity," that which unites, deep down, the diversity of things. The role of link attributed to style is all the more useful when fragmentation and heterogenization are all the more important. To take up once more an idea I have often developed, style, from this point of view, links "with a dotted line" the diverse elements of social reality. Making use of a metaphor borrowed from Freud, one may consider it a sort of "psychic underground," serving as an unconscious substrate of reality in its entirety.

This idea of "underground" is instructive. In fact, numerous societies had a "double," celestial or chthonic, that gave them meaning. In our case, this "double" had been projected by modernity onto a time to come: this was the perfect society or the one to be perfected, which was specific to the diverse sorts of socialisms or capitalisms. This meant one did not need to worry about it in the present, in the here and now. With the bankruptcy of such a projection—already evident for the socialisms, and of which one will soon be aware for the capitalisms—the necessity of such a "double" takes on new importance. This idea, in addition, is found under the most diverse appellations among others than myself: in Jean Duvignaud's "price of priceless things," or the notion of the "immaterial" proposed by Jean-François Lyotard, perhaps even in Jean Baudrillard's analyses of the "simulacrum." In a word, one reaffirms clearly that reality encompasses its opposite, and one can thus understand a "work of negation" that does not resolve itself into a dialectical synthesis: the material having more and more need of the spiritual, the physical no longer being able to be understood without the metaphysical, and the corporal taking on meaning only as a function of the mystical.

Daily life gives us profuse examples of these conjunctions, in particular among the young—examples that are also found in institutions, in businesses, and in daily life, where it has now become commonplace to employ spirituality, New Age practices, and other nonrational techniques to reassure, perfect, and accompany the rational objectives of the institutions and businesses in question or quite simply to ameliorate one's personal existence. The whole thematic of the qualitative, of the "in-house ethos" *(l'esprit maison)* and the enterprise culture all testify to the presence, the weight, of the immaterial "double" at the heart of contemporary society. In other words, our societies, in a more-or-less conscious manner, are themselves preoccupied with this famous "holism" that envisages everything in interaction and in its totality.

It is precisely this globalism that one can better analyze and understand thanks to the notion of style, in that it crystallizes totally disparate elements and domains and makes them interact with each other. Here I will refer to the classic definition given by Shapiro: "Style is a manifestation of culture as totality; it is the visible sign of its unity. Style reflects or projects the 'interior form' of collective thinking and sentiment. What is important here is not the style of an isolated individual or art, but forms or qualities shared by all the arts of a single culture over a significant lapse of time. In is in this sense that one speaks of classical man, medieval man . . ."[7] Here we have all the ingredients of an enlarged conception of style, given as an expression of an epoch and a translation of the state of mind that is its own, whence its usefulness for the framework of a sociological analysis, especially in a period when values are changing. It enables us to stress that which,

far from being anecdotal or marginal, is, in fact, at the very
heart of the nascent sociality and constitutes its kernel. In *De
Ordine*, which one can consider as a treatise on style, Saint
Augustine declares that "human reason is a force that tends
to unity." The formula is synthetic, of a perfect classicism,
and well demonstrates how the fact of stylizing, of looking
for a common denominator, comes down to making use of
reason. Here, also, is what can relativize the overserious spirit
of an orthodox sociology that tends to consider as frivolous
any speculative study bearing on the fruitfulness of the imaginary. Nothing is a stranger to reason, especially not that
which is not reasonable. Or, to borrow expressions dear to
Max Weber and Wilfred Pareto: the nonrational is not irrational, just as the nonlogical is not illogical. The search for social
style is an illustration of this thesis in that it is engaged in finding the internal, embryonic reason, the organic solidarity of
all those elements, be they ever so minute, that the mecha-
nisms of modernity had until now kept separate.

Thus, according to the distinction between culture and civilization characteristic of German thought, style, as a force of
aggregation, would be the property of culture in its founding
inception.[8] It is what at a determined moment assures the synthesis of values and thereby imposes a recognizable order and
form. These days one observes it in all domains, from the
most frivolous to the most serious, in which social life is concerned with "putting into form" *(mise en forme)*. It might
mean the body that is constructed, the individual appearance
that is groomed, the effort spent at presenting the production
of ideas well, the industrial product about to be aestheticized,
the business whose public image is nursed, or even the political program to be presented with all the exterior attractive-
ness possible. In all these, there is a "cultural" concern, a syn-

thetic effort that considers that the product, the body, the idea, the program, or whatever is a globality, or even that its "internal content" cannot exist without its "external shape."

It will be necessary to return to this point, but one can already say that after the cultural moment that was the birth of bourgeois values—from the Lutheran free will to the French Revolution, via the Cartesian subject and the Rousseauian social contract—bourgeois ideology was gradually transformed into a civilization of utility, even a form of "implementarianism." This utilitarian civilization, of which the "primacy of economics" is the ultimate expression, contaminated everything, up to and including those people who held it in contempt. In this respect, the passage of the Communist countries to a market economy, and the conversion of socialists, or social democrats, to the hard laws of realistic management, are phenomena that give food for thought. They could also provoke some smiles, since the apogee of a civilization is very often the sign of its ending. And the very people who underwent this slow or abrupt conversion would be well inspired by being attentive to the prevailing wind *(l'air du temps)*, which, via many clues, seems to announce a new metamorphosis.

In short, the concern with form of which I have spoken, another way of saying the force of style, well expresses the aesthetic paradigm of postmodernity: the birth of a new founding moment, the emergence of a new culture. The languishing civilization of an economic and utilitarian modernity is being succeeded by a new culture in which the sense of the superfluous, the concern for the useless, and the search for the qualitative all take on paramount importance. The stylistic impulse as a manner of thinking, acting, and feeling is the clearest index of this. One should not attribute this tendency just to the developed countries. In specific modulations, one also finds it in so-called developing countries. There, the affirmation of traditional ways of being and the accentuation of local customs and forms of communitarian solidarity will be the mark of the aesthetic I have just described. It is an aesthetic that cannot be reduced to art but that connects with shared emotions and sentiments lived in common. Thus, style as an ensemble of ordered forms, experienced as such, is a contemporaneous characteristic that is now widespread. This very thing is cause and effect of the sociality being born at this century's end.

Too often, in fact, we have a tendency to consider that which belongs to the immaterial sphere as a simple effect of fashion *(mode)*, as something that is in essence vaporous, meaning fleeting—what the law of reality can (and will) sweep away in a gust of wind. This is why my remarks are dedicated to inverting this perspective and showing that style, far from being a "superstructure" determined by a much more solid infrastructure, in fact refers back to a truly general conception of life, conditioning the set of religious, political, and economic institutions of a given period.

That one may have a hard time taking such an inversion into account is not surprising: the very notion of style is limited to an epoch and does not pretend to eternity. Moreover, this is the paradox of the notion: on the one hand, one may present it as a general conception of life, while on the other, it concerns a conception that is deliberately lived in the present and in no way aspires to last.

Goethe saw in paradox the dynamic aspect of a culture in its nascent state. From this viewpoint, the emphasis placed on style is the clue illuminating a cultural renaissance touching all aspects of daily life. The effervescence it induces could perhaps even lead us to speak of a new cultural renaissance, so important is the ideological and existential change. It is easy, and sometimes somewhat facile, to speak incessantly of a Copernican revolution or an epistemological break, but in this case the chasm existing between what is experienced by the mainstream and what is (so badly) thought through by or-

thodox sociology or philosophy is such that one must, with no
fear whatsoever, use such expressions. One can apply to social
life what was said about the redefinition of style by Flaubert:
it is an absolutely other way of seeing things, the shift from an
aesthetic of representation to an aesthetic of perception.

Hans Robert Jauss, who makes this analysis, speaks of
"pure visual sensitivity" or of the "deconceptualization of the
world." In this perspective, it is less a question of dominating
the world by the concept than of assuring its "spiritual mastery" by visual pleasure. "Aesthetic perception thus understood should proceed only from a deconceptualization of the
world, and wants to reveal things shorn of all that which over-
loads their pure visual appearance."[9] In other words, if one remains with this literary example, style shifts from an "activist" conception of the social world to another, based more on
sensuous enjoyment, through the expedient of the image, because of the importance that form is going to assume. Even if
it is banal to recall it, one cannot avoid indicating how the
multiplication of images, their daily omnipresence, illustrates
this thesis. The image is consumed, collectively, in the here
and now. It serves as an aggregative factor; it permits us to
perceive the world and not to represent it. And even if one
could recuperate it from a political point of view, it has above
all a mythological function: it favors mystery; that is, it unites
the initiated one to another.

It is such an initiation that could lead us to say that the aesthetic paradigm is anything but individualist—or rather that
individuals are worth less in themselves than as a function
of the groups to which they are aggregated. From this we understand what, despite their differences, might unite Botti-
celli and Lorenzo de Credi, what could differentiate a Floren-
tine painter from a Venetian one, and how the Dutchmen
Hobbema and Ruysdael, as dissimilar as they seem, share

many things in common, by comparison with a Flemish painter such as Rubens. Heinrich Wölfflin goes so far as to speak of a "style of the school, the country, the race."[10] The expression is strong and well translates, in a metaphoric manner, the new form of sociality induced by style. Whether one regrets it or not, it is truly a "time of the tribes" that is thus beginning, a time in which the style of seeing, feeling, loving, or being enthusiastic together and in the present wins out, without encountering any opposition, over rational representations oriented toward the future.

As a consequence, style becomes a sort of common language—even and especially if what is "in common" is shared only by a few. Moreover, there is a familiar expression, tautological and bordering on a gurgle—an expression used by certain groups of French adolescents—that well translates this tribalism: "style like . . . " *(style genre . . .)*. For example, one says that someone is or does something *style genre* ("in a style kind of like so-and-so . . . "). By this interjection one signals that someone participates, or wants to participate, in such a group, fashion, or mode of being or thinking. And it is well understood that this adherence is displayed by a stereotypical, even coded, language. Here language serves as password, as sign of recognition, and allows groups sharing the same "style like" to aggregate outside the limits of their territory (zone, school, relations of friendship). Studies of young people's vacations and the type of sociability they induce demonstrate clearly that this is how, a priori and without foundations, juvenile attractions and repulsions are formed, during summer periods in particular.

This is why it is better to speak of style not as a language, but rather "as speech" *(parole)* in its strongest sense, that is, as what makes up society, which has an internal order and logic, with the whole expressing itself in specific rituals and fashioning the whole of daily life. I have indicated as much earlier with regard to collective "genius": run-of-the-mill life, life without quality, through its most anodyne moments, and its situations apparently without great significance, becomes a perpetual creation, even and especially if it is not projected onto a distant ideal, but is lived in the present and in a place that I share with others. The accentuation of localism, the search for merging, the pleasure of being together without purpose or use, tribal mimeticism, the conformisms of thought, habit, and dress—all are there to prove it and can be given nuance, refined, or concealed, according to strata or social appearances. One can live it in a more-or-less open manner, but the tendency is both undeniable and widespread: one lives, along with other people, styles that constitute all of us in depth. To put it differently, style is above all the fact of existing only and through the look or the word of the other.

From such a perspective, one cannot be content with saying "style makes the man." Or else we should give this expression its widest meaning: man is what he partakes of the general, the typical, the extrapolatable and characteristic. In fact, the notion of style teaches us that a person is only such when he or she is rooted in a substratum that gives each its value, that he or she is only worth something within the framework of his or her social and natural environment. I borrow a fine expression from Julien Gracq that speaks of "the bedrock of culture from which the works of our times grow and are nourished." He goes on to specify that this "bedrock of culture" in no way bridles personal originality but, on the contrary, "maintains" it, "lays out its terrain." The bedrock, let us not forget, is what gives things foundation; it is a capital, an ensemble of qualities, and also can be—if one may use a culinary metaphor—that from which a sauce is going to take, the dish turn out fine and be appreciated.

This is what allows us to cross the bridge that pits base *(fond)* against form as opposing alternatives: in fact, there is constant interaction between the two and, as far as we are concerned, a person's form is not possible unless it is rooted in a collective wellspring. This is the common "bedrock" that allows artists of an era to be what they are. It is also that which determines the different attitudes, exceptional or banal, of social life. One glimpses the whole sociological interest there could be in using the dialectic existing between base and form, and of which style is the expression. Whatever the term used— the ideal type (Weber), residue (Pareto), essential character (Durkheim), structure (Lévi-Strauss), archetype (Durand)— the essential thing is to bring out a common denominator capable, if not of explaining an epoch in its totality, at least of sketching its principal contours. From this viewpoint, style is a chosen methodological lever: it accentuates, enlarges, caricatures, and thus brings out what tends, too often, to be neglected, out of moralistic habit.

Paroxysm, even what is shocking about it, is quite revealing. Each individual—but also each epoch—as Emile Cioran reminds us, possesses "reality only by his exaggerations, by his capacity to overestimate."[11] This is just the reality that concerns us, and style, in what is excessive about it, is a good means of reaching it. It is like a musical base from which particular situations and behaviors detach themselves, a leitmotiv of a recurrent theme that both unifies different scatterings and allows us to establish kinship among all the heterogeneous elements of a fragmented society. One could compare it to Vinteuil's sonata in Proust: a musical line thanks to which the becoming and the permanent are conjugated. The whole Proustian novel rests on variations and changes (if not contradictions), and the little sonata, in its haunting aspect, recollects what is constant.

One could ramble on infinitely with such a metaphor. It suffices to indicate it as a key idea recalling that repetitions and redundancies of style underline ad nauseam that there are epochs in which, instead of opposing each other, the static and the dynamic enter into synergy. At certain times, as was the case in traditional societies, the static won out, and only references to space, to form, to territory, to the body had importance. There are other times, including modernity, in which the dynamic predominates. In this case, only history, development, growth, the future, and their diverse consequences are taken into account and serve as points of reference for the different rational constructions that justify them. There is a third case, under which one might put postmodernity, which simultaneously stresses invariants, constants, and what is static about them, yet does not neglect modulations and variations, with their dynamic energy. It is this conjunction that we find in style, which is a sort of "Einsteinized" time, a time that is concentrated, spatialized, and which, through the rites and other forms of daily customs, allows us to enjoy, as well as can be expected, the world as it is.

So there is in the stylization of existence something that goes back to relativism. But the latter should not be understood solely as the absence of conviction or ideal. Closer to its etymology, one could say that it puts things into relation with each other: relation with space, and with the earth—ecology is the clearest indication of it these days—but also with other people. After Aristotle and Saint Thomas Aquinas, and before others such as Mauss and more recently Bourdieu, Spengler spoke of the "important concept" of *habitus*. In particular he showed that the habitus of a plant is the specific manner it has of accommodating itself to its environment, which is another way of saying its enrootedness (static), while marking its specificity in developing itself and growing (dynamic). Then, as he applied it to the great organisms of history, he realized that the "some vague inkling [of habitus] has always . . . underlain the notion of *style* . . . this 'habit' of existence in space, which covers, in the case of the individual, action and thought and conduct and disposition, embraces in the case of the existence of whole cultures the totality of life-expressions of the higher order."[12]

The ramifications that Spengler drew from this are fascinating, because he showed that it is this that conditions forms of spiritual communication, the type of dress, government, communication and news circulation. In extrapolating his remarks, and in becoming attentive to the specific social rhythm induced by the conjunction of which I have spoken, one may recall that through style, each individual, each particular element of the given mundane world, crystallizes the whole epoch. Evidently there exist typical figures—Parsifal, Faust, Werther, Byron—but it is only after the fact that they become such. And without overstretching the analogy, one could say that it is the same today, except that typical figures, with the help of the media, are felt as such in real time. Thus some sports star or rock singer, some business executive or television celebrity, some intellectual or religious guru, even the star animal of the weekly horse races, will (for a while) crystallize the collective genius. By means of this crystallization, microcommunities will be constituted. And this may explain the saturation of the democratic ideal and the emergence, ambiguous in many respects, of what one may call the communitarian ideal.

The Transmutation of Values

Progressively, the imaginary that modernity could consider as being of the order of the superfluous or of frivolity tends to find once again a place of honor in social life. One could ad-

vance the hypothesis that what is true of the human being applies to the social body. The former, in effect, when it has
made a large expenditure that is purely cerebral or physical,
has need of "releasing" itself and is engaged more or less un-
consciously in regaining its equilibrium by playing on its potentialities for fantasy and its oneiric and ludic faculties. This
is the compensatory role that free time, leisure, or other forms
of "vacation" for the mind and body may play. The pioneer-
ing work of Joffre Dumazedier and a great deal of contemporary research on "nonconstrained" time are instructive in this
respect. In pushing the analysis a little further, it is possible to
ask whether, after having been subject to the harsh laws of
productivity, after having been dominated by the reality principle of the "primacy of economics," societies are not on the
way to rediscovering the charms of relaxation, or at the very
least the relativization of the activism that has marked the
past two centuries.

Once we admit such a hypothesis, we need not wonder at
the revival of the imaginary. From a holistic perspective, the
latter restores a lost equilibrium, both by reinvesting in archaic structures that had been thought superseded and by rec-
reating mythologies that are going to serve as social link. The
explosion of images proves this. Thanks to them, societies
dream and thus recuperate a part of themselves of which they
were defrauded by an essentially rationalist modernity. Nor
should we be surprised that this revival, like the return of the
repressed, takes place in a somewhat disorganized manner
and may be, in many respects, excessive. All periods of passage are effervescent and have need of a little time to redis-
cover an equilibrium upset by the intrusion of new structures.

It is by bearing this in mind that one may comprehend the
transmutations in style observable these days, in which style
tends, after being merely utilitarian, to shift to integrating all

the aesthetic dimensions (oneiric, ludic, symbolic) whose effects may be constantly seen in daily life. Historians of thought, when they identify transitional periods, take note of changes in tone among the authors typical of an epoch. Thus a certain warmth, a certain "impetus," an original accent has been noticed in the work of Pico della Mirandola, or else a "new timbre" characterizing Erasmus's contribution. Such imagistic expressions well translate the emotional, affective, and sensible aspects of works participating in the change in question, which considerably outstrips the simple rational dimension. Certainly there may be modifications of the concepts translating or legitimating this change, but sentiment and the culture that it fosters occupy the most important place in them.

Myth is a totality and would not be reduced to a simple rational dimension, and so in order to gain access to this new totality that is emerging, it is necessary to rely on experience and how it partakes of the sensible, in that it puts all the components of the human or social being into play. To take another literary example, it is striking to observe that, underlining the typical aspect of Jünger's novel *On the Marble Cliffs,* Julien Gracq notes the "particular timbre" of the novelist's voice and style, the latter being cause and effect of the typicality represented by the novel. So he says of the novel in question: "our epoch is its subject matter, but the internal coherence" comes from the fact that "everything there is transmuted."[13]

The remark is limpid and may help us think through the specificity of style that is being sketched out before us. The different constitutive elements of modernity are not "superseded," in the dialectical sense of the term; nor are they finished, as it is too often the custom to say. In fact, one cannot deny that they continue to play a role in social life, but imperceptibly they take on another timbre, and their tonality is no

longer the same. In an alchemical manner, they have under-
gone a sort of transmutation and, while remaining what they
are, they will make up another configuration. To cite but one
example, scientific or technological development not only
continues to exist, but even goes on developing, and yet its
meaning is no longer the same. Thus personal computers and
the Minitel videotext in France or the Internet, whose futuris-
tic aspects cannot be denied and which represents the spear-
head of this development, are no longer only the vectors of a
totally technologized society, but tend to favor *proxemic*
communication. They are inscribed in a context in which the
ludic and the dream are not absent. By this fact they foster a
symbolic style of life, that is, a style of exchange and communication in which the immaterial and—why not use the
word?—the *mystical* play a role that is not negligible. These
latter are even more present and meaningful in that they are
no longer projected onto a celestial background or onto one
to come later, but, on the contrary, are lived in the immediacy
of daily life. And it is not surprising to notice how, in a related
manner, programmers who are totally competent in their field
may be, at the same time, frenzied adepts of the New Age and
practice parapsychology or be interested in alternative medicines. What I have just said about computing may be applied
to many other fields just as characteristic of our era. It is in
this sense that we can speak of transmutation.

Nevertheless we should note that such a transmutation is
never brutal or total. The mythology being born does so only
gradually. Most often it is superimposed over previous myths,
which continue, in certain sectors, to exercise real influence.
Hence the style of an epoch may be simultaneously "evident"
to those who live it and totally opaque to those who try to analyze it. There is a beautiful metaphor used by Gilbert Durand
that is quite illuminating for our topic, that of the "semantic

basin." Like a hydrographic process, an ideology is progressively constituted by a multitude of trickling runoffs that down in the valley are going to result in a watercourse that will be given a name after the fact, then be canalized, before losing itself in the meanderings of the delta and being thrown into the sea, thus giving birth to a new cycle.

The metaphor is suggestive, as are the historical examples that Durand offers to illustrate this mechanism: Franciscanism in the eighteenth century and the life philosophy during the romantic period. Thanks to this metaphor we can suddenly perceive how, by successive sedimentations, contemporary myths are elaborated: there are fragments of myths, or whole myths, on standby, unused in the framework of social consensus, that represent the strange, the marginal, the exceptional; then other myths are taken up by thinkers that are going to become the consensus of the era, as the whole mixes with the mythic remains of the era that is coming to an end, relics that may be made use of on different occasions.[14] This well describes the emergence of a new style, how it is composed of different ingredients that one can empirically notice, and which are best expressed in the numerous contradictory situations and attitudes that punctuate everyday life.

It is, in fact, common to pinpoint attitudes regarding sex, relation to work, or ideology—mind-sets that may appear totally discordant from each other. So, for example, marriage endures and conjugal or family life is elaborated according to the most traditional norms, but at the same time, the man or woman who lives this may go in for diverse perversions that morality reproves or, quite simply, may live a diversity of relations at the same time, without an overly bad conscience. The same is true concerning work, where one may be an efficient and industrious employee and at the same time have other centers of interest or a whole series of ruses and loopholes to make this work bearable. We could say the same thing about different ideological convictions that very quickly become worn out, to which one adheres and yet rejects without many scruples. In each case, we may observe a series of successive sincerities, which is really the mark of a lifestyle made up of odds and ends, of a style consisting of totally diverse contributions—all of which are symptomatic of transitional periods.

In a previous book *(Aux Creux des Apparences)* I have shown that this "chameleon" attitude can be explained by the saturation of the identity principle and the emergence of the successive identifications characteristic of postmodernity. For his part, the philosopher Gilbert Simondon speaks of "non-identity of a being in relation to itself." And to explain this he offers the notion of *transduction*, "the physical, biological, mental, social operation by which an activity propagates itself step by step into the interior of a [specific] domain." According to Simondon, transduction starting from the center of a being extends in different directions and thereby expresses the multiple dimensions of the being.[15]

Such a logical and philosophical definition is quite pertinent for grasping the mechanism of transmutation of a social style that it, too, is gradually diffracted and simultaneously affects different domains, situations, and structures of existence—from the physical to the social, via the mental, and the different facets of the individual being. Indeed, style applies to the physical exterior. Fashion, dress, and gestures all prove this. But it is equally found in diverse representations, language practices, and the ideological uniformities of a given moment. Finally, it does not fail to act within the globality of the social. The formation of crystal, as Simondon indicates, is the clearest image to take account of the contaminating effect of style. From a very small germ the crystal grows, and it extends itself in all directions in its supersaturated water base, then each layer serves as the base for the formation of the next one. The result is a structure in the form of a network.

It is the same, as I have just said, with the constitution of myth, and hence of the style that expresses it. It is by successive layers, starting from an existing germ, that they take shape and that they are gradually diffracted. Let us note that their formation and diffraction take place when there is, and because there is, saturation of an existing state. Here perhaps is the only social "law" that it is possible to offer within the social sciences: it is the saturation of a cultural ensemble, as Sorokin has well demonstrated, that allows other forms to be born. The whole interest in style is to make us attentive to the crystallization that this mechanism induces. And since we have referred to metaphors from hydrology, mineralogy, and physics, we might say that this crystallization is widespread in social experience and that while it is often totally misrecognized (or denied) by established knowledge, it is more experimental and empirical than conceptual.

In fact, contrary to conventional thought, which judges style as a measure of the superfluous, there is in the latter something that is, above all and essentially, concrete. To take up a definition from the catechism: on the model of the sacraments, it makes visible an invisible grace. Put otherwise, it sees itself and—I repeat—it makes perceptible more than it represents. But we have difficulty freeing ourselves from the philosophy of representation. Style gives form to, puts into form, expresses itself in *images*—all that comes down to the concrete at its most evident, lived, and experienced. It is just this that makes style a contemporary notion. The saturation of a political that is, in essence, distant and projective gives back to the quotidian and to relations of "proximity" all their importance. What was to come, what was only hoped for in the future framework of a perfect society, or one to be per-

fected, now becomes visible, possible, and even palpable. This
is what I have called the *transfiguration of the political*. It
gives way to the domestic, with the culture of sentiment as its
most visible expression.

Style is both cause and effect of such a process. Specifically,
it allows us to remember that this concrete, this quotidian, this
banal life without quality—all things that were largely mini-
mized, if not devalorized, throughout modernity—are inverting into their contraries. Or, more exactly, they give birth to
what they were bearing. The spiritual arises from the material:
hence the mystical images that will be used to account for this
inversion. Hence, too, the fact that religiosity is something increasingly widespread in social existence. One could refer to
an analysis by Lou Andreas-Salomé, whose free spirit and
nonconformity we know and who did not hesitate, alongside
perfectly rationalist reflections, to use religious metaphors to
account for the richness and subtlety of life. So, to account for
the synergy of which I have just spoken—that of the material
and the spiritual—she made reference to the process by which
"the vast universal matrix of physiology spawns psychic life."
And to illustrate this, she did not shrink from speaking of the
"transubstantiation" of the bread and wine in Catholic theology, which is, as we know, a sacrament of union, noting that
"there are things that can only be grasped when stylized."[16]

Once again we are confronted with a paradoxical thought.
It is a paradox that cuts across—as I have indicated on several
occasions—all those contemporary phenomena resting on the
conjunction of opposing, if not contradictory, attitudes. In
this respect the style of juvenile behaviors is more and more
instructive: it simultaneously allies a very palpable hedonism
and a perfectly idealistic generosity, an affected casualness in
relation to certain established values and a search for authenticity in behaviors, the concern for original creation and the

sharpest contempt for all repetitive work. One could, at leisure, extend the list of these attitudes that, if taken as a function of a purely rational logic, may appear incoherent, but, if
one is attentive to the paradoxical dynamic of all nascent culture, instead testify to a global (holistic) perception of life, in
which good and evil, shadow and light, are conjugated in a
creative synergy.

It suffices, in this respect, to refer to all the charitable deeds
cropping up these days, to the multiplicity of musical concerts
organized in order to finance some noble cause, to all the
daily small acts of solidarity, to the different forms of generosity at the heart of urban "tribes," or to voluntary work within
the framework of multiple associations, in order to grasp the
style of postmodern life. It is a mistake to lament the individualistic narrowing, the egotism, the loss of civic responsibility
that are supposed to prevail these days. In fact, what I call the
style of the "communitarian ideal" cannot be measured by
the standards of the political project of modernity. More precisely, it blows this project wide open, turns it into a mockery,
or else regards it only with indifference. But this does not
mean that another type of solidarity is not being born—rather
the contrary. It is an organic solidarity, in its strongest meaning, that is coming forth—a solidarity that holds together all
the elements that modernity had dismembered, an organicism
that, in a more lived than conceptualized fashion, engages the
totality of the person in the familiar communitarian framework (tribe, group, clan, etc.), and in which that person can
invest himself or herself in actions close at hand, or at the very
least in actions having direct repercussions on the community
itself. In effect, the majority of charitable actions of which we
have just spoken have no tangible result whatsoever, or else
very mediocre results, if one measures them by the standard
of the instrumental reason of efficacy. On the other hand, they

favor communal emotion, they comfort collective sentiment, and, by this fact, they fortify the communitarian link.

This is how the transmutation of values engenders another social style, that is, another relation to alterity: the Other is no longer an abstraction, with which I must unite in order to construct a no less abstract, future society. The other is the one I touch and with whom I make something that touches me. It is this tactile style—which owes something to the baroque, as has been shown—that is cause and effect of the organicism referred to previously. One would be well advised, in order to understand sociality in these times (or even to act on it), to be attentive to this emotional ambience, to discern the outline of an affective activity that, though showing neither finality nor particular purpose, no less denotes one of the most original social creations.

This creation, which escapes the activist logic proper to modernity, is in many respects hidden, secret, and mysterious. It does not allow itself to be apprehended by the instruments of analysis currently used by sociologists, but it is no less strong and solid for that. Although being nonactive within it, it "makes society." It is this paradox that we must address head-on. To do this, we must remember that there can exist an "ethical aesthetic." Though these two terms are very often disconnected and cover separate domains, numerous historians of ideas have shown that there have been societies and cultures in which they were perfectly conjoined. Similarly, I have offered the hypothesis (in *Aux Creux des Apparences*) that the postmodernity that is appearing skirts relying on an "ethic of the aesthetic"—nothing else than a social creation that is at once both nonactive and the product of these new forms of emotional and affective solidarities to which I have just referred.

If one pushes the hypothesis a little further, one could equally say that the transmutation that is at issue here is, in part, the result of the conjunction between the aesthetic and the mystical. Or, to put it another way, the fact of feeling collective emotions, the fact that creation may be less an action than a communal passion (which is proper to the aesthetic)—all this favors communitarian sentiment. The mystical is that which unites the initiated (sharing a mystery) one to another. I know that I am being heavy-handed, as I often am when I propose analyzing some form of paroxysm. Nevertheless, one could say that mystical experience, in the sense I have just indicated, is one of the vectors of contemporary sociality: creative not-doing is the very thing that comforts a being-togetherness that is self-sufficient, having no need of nor searching for particular objectives to justify itself. It is what one could call a sociality without purpose or finality. This is what, beyond the thematic of representation (political or philosophical), makes aesthetic contemplation come together with mystical contemplation. Contrary to what happens within the framework of the social contract or the democratic ideal, the world is no longer to be transformed, or perfected; society and history are no longer to be made. Rather the opposite: natural and social environments are accepted for what they are; it suffices to accommodate oneself to them, and to try, in an ecological manner, to draw the most possible benefits from them. It is in this sense that one could understand them as being, in the narrow meaning of the term, a matrix that is cause and effect of the communitarian ideal.

Such a perspective was widespread in the many artistic avant-gardes, surrealism in particular, between the two world wars. But, on the one hand these avant-gardes remained partly "contaminated" by the activist mythologies of the moment (namely, Marxism), and on the other hand they involved only very small groups. It would seem these days that the style supposed by these artistic avant-gardes may have in-

filtrated the whole of the body social, and that nothing or nobody may escape it. "It is not fortuitous that a fashion, a system of thought, a way of living or a refusal to live, is found in
the mood of the times." Roger Vailland's formula, taken from
his book on surrealism, *Le Regard Froid,* well illustrates this
hypothesis, with the corrective that I have offered: this "spirit
of the times" is no longer the prerogative of a few, or it is no
longer imposed on the great mass by a few. On the contrary, it
is widely lived, "perceived" by the social ensemble, and very
little "represented" by those whose profession is to observe
and analyze or by those who are in a position to decide for
this social ensemble.

From this one clearly perceives the amplitude of the transmutation and, at the same time, in what way the notion of
style is an instrument of choice for apprehending it. As is often the case, the novelist more than the theoretician hastens
the change, and this precisely because he or she is sensitive to
the sensible. Thus, speaking only of one of the greatest of this
century, James Joyce does not want to "create a fictional mythology beyond the world he represents, but rather tries to
conjure up the world's essence, or its essential horror, by
mythifying it, as it were, through the stylistic principle" as
Theodor Adorno says.[17] And we know with what felicity and
what acuity he managed to do so, since it is true that each
character in *Ulysses* and the book as a whole are specific
"types" and typical of their epoch. The "stylistic principle" is
a felicitous and pertinent expression. It takes account of the
fact that in all domains—artistic but also those concerning
daily life—style finds its origin in the most interior region of
creation. It is an ordering principle. Because it leads to the visible, by making present, it fosters symbolism in its simplest
sense, meaning that by which society is what it is.

Style, visibility or appearance, ordering principle—here we

have the diverse active moments (not to be understood in chronological fashion) in the elaboration of a culture. This is also what allows us to understand the passage from one style to another. Or, more precisely, it is what makes style, after having been neglected throughout modernity, take on the contemporaneous importance we now know, since it stresses the play of forms, the role of appearance, of which the omnipresent image and the prevalence of "the look" are the most informative indices. At the same time, it induces new, autonomous ways of being, and other ways of behaving toward others—things that refer back to the ordering principle. The fact that values die does not mean that all values are dead. Despite (or because of) what may appear frivolous, superficial, a pure play of appearance, there is in postmodern style a social order being sketched out—on which it behooves us now to insist, because it is from such an order that a sociality is developing, whose profundity, to borrow an expression of Nietzsche's, should be sought on the surface of things.

An Aesthetic Style

What could be the essential characteristic of the style arising from the transmutation of values that has taken place over several decades and is on the way to completion at the century's end? As I have indicated on several occasions, in a more-or-less precise manner, it is a way of being aesthetic that tends to prevail in our societies. However, let us be precise that the said aesthetic has nothing to do with the one that can be confined to the fine arts: it encompasses them, but also extends to the whole of social existence—life as a work of art, in some sense, or else the aesthetic as a way of feeling and experiencing in common. Empirically, this sends us back to all the forms of gatherings—musical, sporting, consuming, religious

—that, although they have always existed, in certain epochs find (or recover) an amplitude that they had lost or that had been relativized. This explains why the aesthetic no longer inevitably obeys the different criteria of good taste elaborated during the era of bourgeois dominance and now asserts itself essentially as a vector of sociality, a way of enjoying together an eternal present. It is that which is recognized in the somewhat paradoxical expression "mystical materialism." It is made up of hedonism, of bodies, of objects, of images, of space—with all that these partake of the concrete—but is then transmuted into mysticism, that is to say, is shared, and thus favors a mysterious union or, nearer to its etymology, a *communion.*

Without reading too much into the texts, one could refer to this passage from the Epistle to the Romans in which Saint Paul remarks that "for all that may be known of God by men lies plain before their eyes" (Rom. 1:19–20). Starting from here, it is therefore possible to offer an enlarged interpretation of the aesthetic as a process of "correspondence," as much with the social environment as with the natural environment. This is a cosmic "correspondence" that, overcoming the usual separation specific to modernity, makes each and every part a necessary and reversible element in an ordered globality. In this sense the material universe, the worldly given, is traversed, through and through, by an immaterial force—whatever name one may give to the latter. The ambient ecology and religiosity are the clearest indices of such a conjunction, a conjunction that, as has been often stressed, is very close to the romantic spirit of which one finds numerous manifestations in contemporary style, and that (though it displeases those who are obsessed by the politicoeconomic reality principle) is observed not only among the younger generations but equally among numerous strata, classes, or socioprofessional categories. To summarize this tendency in one phrase, one might speak of what Mikhail Bakunin called an "invisible collective force" that is at the origin, according to him, of the regular explosive revolts punctuating human histories, but that one could equally well find at work in the calm relaxation of a life without quality.[18]

Thus, then, the aesthetic style, in making us attentive to the globality of things, to the reversibility of different elements of this globality, is at the conjunction of the material and the immaterial and tends to favor a being-togetherness not seeking an objective to attain, not oriented to the future, but engaged quite simply in enjoying the good things of this world, in cultivating what Michel Foucault called the "care for the self" or the "use of pleasures," in seeking, within the reduced framework of tribes, to meet another person and share with him a few common emotions and sentiments. In the cyclical balancing of social values, we witness the return to the communitarian ideal, to the detriment of the societal ideal. Such a communitarian impulse is found in what I have called postmodern tribalism, whose effects make themselves felt as much in juvenile effervescences as in the multiplication of aggregations developed on the basis of sexual, cultural, religious, or even political tastes. These aggregations no longer owe anything to rational programming, but rather rely on the desire to be with similar-minded people, even it it means excluding those who are different. This "homosociality" predominates in all domains, and it leaves nothing immune: politics becomes a story of clans; the university or the press is fragmented into competing and opposed chapels; institutions whatever they may be are split into groups, more or less hostile, very often fighting among each other.

Is this not drawing too bleak a picture of the aesthetic style? Not necessarily, because there is a to-and-fro between attrac-

tion (that of homosociality) and repulsion (that of exclusion),
an exchange that no less leads to a sort of coenesthetic equilibrium. It is a conflictual equilibrium where good and evil, truth
and falsehood, functioning and dysfunctioning manage to
come to terms with each other. By this I mean that these tribes
who most of the time congregate around an eponymous hero
(intellectual or religious gurus, political or economic leaders,
founders of schools of thought, etc.) are obliged to "adjust"
themselves, as well as they can, among each other. Images cir-
culate and confront one another, competing mythologies are
paraded, composite ideologies are patched together by trans-
mission groups—but all this is obliged to take place in copresence and, hence, each has to accommodate the other. In short,
to put it in metaphoric form, speech (meaning image, ideology, mythology) circulates and by this fact, whether one
wishes it or not, engenders a form of "universal sympathy" or
empathy. *Stricto sensu,* one "feels along with, together."

This adjustment can be made in violence, and different rac-
isms, fanaticisms, and urban uprisings are there to prove it,
but it may equally be expressed in tolerance, and many are the
groups that work in this direction; one finds it too, finally, in
indifference, which is perhaps the most widespread case.
Somehow, by the nature of things, this adjustment takes
place. It is the postmodern form of the social link—a social
link "in dotted outline," shaken by violent, chaotic, and un-
foreseen jolts, but the latter thereby no less testify to a solid
organicism. In effect, relativism, induced by tribalism and by
the multiplication of patched-together ideologies or mythologies, calls for a pluralist "composition," structurally and logically. In coming to terms *(composition)* we find the verb compose: one negotiates, one delineates the real or symbolic
territories, and just by this one comes into contact. Thus relativism put things into relations: forced, violent, or aggressive

relations or sometimes, on the contrary, relations of complicity, of alliance, or quite simply of fondness. In any case, it is not isolation, specific to an exacerbated individualism, but, on the contrary, an all-out relationism that predominates within the framework of tribalism.

It is good to keep this in mind in order to appreciate what I call here the aesthetic style. In fact, whether by attraction or repulsion, there is something that pushes me toward or up against the other. So it is in relation to the other that I situate myself. One sees clearly that this forms an antinomy with the modern democratic ideal relying on a conception of the autonomous individual, master of himself and of his history and entering into contractual relations with other autonomous individuals in order to make History and Society. As I have already had occasion to indicate (in *Le Temps des Tribus*), it is fusion, even confusion, that overtakes distinction in the elaboration of a postmodern social link. Certain studies of the cult of the body—bodybuilding, diets, the press and magazines, dress fashion, sporting activities—demonstrate the indubitable way in which one constructs, cares for, and embellishes the body, partly under the gaze of the other, and partly so that it will be seen by the other. So even what might appear as individualism turns out to be, once more, a manifestation of tribal hedonism.

In a metaphoric manner, one could illustrate this by referring to an analysis by Foucault devoted to a few treatises on marriage, in which he shows that "care for the self" is valid only to the extent that if favors a "stylistic of the link." The sovereignty of the self over the self, another way of describing the care of the body, would thus be sited more within the perspective of reciprocity than within a logic of mastery of the other. "The intensification of the care of the self goes along with the valorization of the other." This is what makes

Foucault speak of an "aesthetic of shared pleasures."[19] One finds here something that sends us back to the thematic of sympathy at issue before: aesthetic values are just the conditions for the possibility of a new social link. In this sense the search for pleasure, the epiphanization of the body, the valorization of free time, the preoccupation with the quality of life, and other forms of "care for the self" are valid only to the extent they favor the desire for the other, the pleasure of being with the other. The example quoted shows that such a perspective regularly returns to the fore. To put it in other terms, sometimes an economy of the self dominates, which goes along with an economy of the world, as was the case of modernity. Sometimes, on the contrary, the care that can be taken of one's own body is just a moment, in the sense Georges Bataille gives to the term, of a generalized *expenditure*. It would seem that the cult of the body that we see today may be the expression of such an expenditure.

There are many examples that point in this direction, and daily life offers a quantity of illustrations of this thesis, ranging from the forms of simple sociability that are developed in gyms, to the tight links that are constituted within groups engaging in dangerous sports, via the friendships and relations induced by clubs, group travel, and tours, without forgetting the sentiment of belonging that is cause and effect of the dress fashion and other corporeal, gestural, and linguistic mimeticisms that are indeed the mark of contemporary societies. It may be found that if placed side by side, all these situations end up creating a specific ambience, an encompassing climate that it is difficult to depart from. It is in this sense that one could speak of the style of an epoch: specifically here, an aesthetic style, one that, on the one hand, stresses the sensible and the hedonism that this induces and, on the other hand, supports different forms of sociality.

In giving to the word *culture* its strongest meaning, that of the soil in which social life takes root, one could speak of an aesthetic culture. This means a moment when aesthetic values contaminate the whole of social life, the moment when nothing escapes their influence, even the moment when social differences no longer have great importance. Thus Hermann Broch, with respect to the hedonist attitude that characterized Vienna at the end of the past century, speaks of a "democracy of life."[20] The expression is powerful, but certainly pertinent for describing the transversal efficacy of style. It cuts across the boundary between different classes, social strata, or socioprofessional categories. Style becomes an encompassing ethic that slowly shapes the manner of being and different forms of representation. It is what Nietzsche, just like Oswald Spengler and Georg Simmel, saw clearly when they each tried to define the style of some historical period—because such a style lets nothing escape its grasp.

Moving beyond examples such as those of ancient Greece or fin de siècle Vienna, it is possible to extrapolate the thesis and show that beauty, bodily pleasure, and other immaterial values assure, to borrow an expression of Gilbert Durand's, a "paracletic presence." This means that, like the Holy Spirit, these values illuminate, encompass, and transform those upon whom they weigh. This allows us to underline the "nonactive" aspect that may be attached to such values: we make them much less than they make us. Similarly—and the metaphors of the Holy Spirit and the Pentecost are instructive in this respect—these values are widely diffused across frontiers, even touching whole societies at a given moment. Regarding the baroque, one was thus able to elaborate a theory of "eons" that, in the manner of spirits infiltrating everywhere, are going to define human creation in its diverse manifestations. Nothing escapes this, not even scientific research, which at some point is going to pose some problem or make some discovery that could not have been done previously and inevitably could not be done later. Biologists such as C. H. Waddington or Rupert Sheldrake go so far as to speak of "chreode" (necessary advance) to explain this process.[21] All that I am merely alluding to here summarizes the force of a "type of sensibility" that, following the cycles unfailingly stressed by the historian of ideas, deeply impregnates the whole of social life.

Style is thus the expression of an era, and as such it allows and enables liaison among all the members of a society. I have often suggested that the essential problem posed to the sociologist is to understand how one manages relationships with alterity; how in all domains each and every one of us behaves in relation to the other. It seems that it is the encompassing style that allows us to grasp the outlines of such a relationship—whence comes the necessity of locating its essential characteristics, so true is it, to take up some past examples again, that a classical, baroque, or modern style will determine specific ways of being and thinking. Moreover, the property of theoretical reflection is to stylize a given epoch. It is in this sense that Simmel could remark that what will remain of Marx's work is his having known how to bring out the "economic style" of modernity. And it is true that the nineteenth century, which one could consider the apogee of modern times, was entirely oriented toward economic things, whether the economy of the self or the economy in the strict sense. But gradually bourgeois culture palled into a civilization that had forgotten its founding myth; the economy became abstract and was no longer felt as an encompassing style. Hence, perhaps, what one calls by an all-purpose term, the "crisis"—which is nothing other than the loss of the consciousness that a society has of itself, bringing about the loss of confidence in itself.

This loss of consciousness and confidence in turn brings about a notorious rigidification. All human things have difficulty accepting their finiteness. Institutions, just like friendly and amorous relations, refuse, for as long as possible, that reality which is death. And, very often, they try to endure, even when what they were leaning on is extinct. The same applies to whole civilizations, engaged in surviving the death of their founding myths. We should not forget that one continues to perceive the light of an extinct star long after its death. As for what regards modernity, the aforementioned rigidification will be expressed in resentment, if not denial. In fact, this will consist in refusing any importance to style or, more exactly, of attributing to it a secondary place and making of it, at best, a "supplement of the soul" for private use or, at worst, a frivolity good only for cheering up the bourgeoisie or justifying the existence of an artistic bohemia.

It is thus that one could explain the distrust, even hostility, of the "establishment" toward the aesthetic style that profoundly informs basic sociality. Under the pretext of being attached to the core, one neglects form, meanwhile forgetting that the form is the very thing, precisely, that expresses, at best, the "base" of being-togetherness. All of Simmel's thought on form rests on this intuition. It is also what Adorno expressed when he remarked, criticizing Georg Lukács, that "stylistic indifference is almost always a symptom of dogmatic rigidification of the content."[22] Now dogmatism is indeed the clearest index of aging, of sclerosis, even of the death of an institution, an ideology, a human relation. In straining to attach oneself to the instituted, one cannot, will not, appreciate life in its nascent state.

This nascent state is always expressed in an untidy and disordered manner. It is always anomic. This entails, within orthodoxy of whatever kind, an accentuation of the normative

attitude that renders it incapable of grasping the dynamic of a
form of new life. Art historians have well analyzed this process, showing that, quite often, one judges a nascent style
with the canons of the one that is dominant. So it is not surprising that this style is perceived by social observers as something dangerous, noxious, uncivilized. Certainly it is so in
many respects, but it is useless to vituperate what is there in
any case. At best, one will consider this style, the efflorescence
of images that express it, or the omnipresence of a form, as
something minor or decadent. In doing so, one overlooks this
"autonomous life of forms" that regularly recurs in the
course of human histories.

In short, the tightening around seriousness, the reality principle, theoretical and ideological dogmatism, and the prevalence of the economic or the political is a rearguard combat.
The multiform moralism that this induces, and that does not
spare even intellectuals (or no longer spares them), is not in
tune any more with a social life that, in multiple ways, escapes
the injunctions of "the duty of being." In fact—and it is this
one may essentially retain from the aesthetic style—the mood
of the time is toward the relativization of utilitarianism. And
the more one is engaged in valorizing the importance of work,
the more one tries to bring free thought into line, the more one
directs education, schools, and universities toward an excessive professionalization, the more one stresses long-term projects, the more one encourages a "utensilitarian" conception
of existence, then the more, as if in response, a sociality asserts
itself, one that, on the contrary, rests on the imaginary, on an
existential casualness, a search for hedonism, a shared pleasure in living, and on appearance and the play of forms. The
list of these attitudes would be long, attitudes with which one
is empirically confronted in ordinary life and that are engaged
in valorizing what Jean Duvignaud called "the price of things

without price." The fact is that relativization of utilitarianism is indeed the mark of the nascent style. It is the index of a kind of social availability that experiments with new ways of being and that seeks other founding myths. Thus, since those who manage the social seem incapable of doing so, it is important that those who are engaged in thinking it through be up to the challenge offered by a life without quality.

Nevertheless, one should specify that hedonism, proper to the aesthetic style, is by no means an individualistic affair. The search for an egotistical happiness is a modern preoccupation, more precisely an occupation of the declining bourgeois civilization. What is being sketched in the nascent culture is the emergence of a shared and tribal happiness. I have already indicated elsewhere the resemblance that seemed to exist between postmodernity and the baroque. Here one may suggest briefly in what way the comparison can be instructive for our thesis. The baroque—architectural, pictorial, musical—was boosted by the Jesuits to magnify the communitarian spirit against the triumphant individualism of the Protestant Reformation. In particular, it has been noted that the decoration and the ornamentation of baroque churches had the function of giving a foretaste of celestial beatitude. But the latter, we must not forget, is essentially communitarian. The exacerbated luxuriousness of these churches, the musical accompaniment, the ambience they secreted, were intended to give rise to a religious pleasure, in the strict meaning of the term, that of *religare,* of linking, of putting into relation. The only happiness that is valued, the happiness of the blessed, happiness without end, is the happiness that one enjoys in common. From this point of view, the baroque is indeed a visible expression of an invisible force: that of the communitarian ideal.

Commenting on what Benedetto Croce says about the baroque age, Eugenio d'Ors, in his celebrated essay, makes a dis-

tinction that may be useful to us here. He shows in effect that
there are "historical styles" and "cultural styles."[23] The former are limited to a particular manifestation, as with the
Gothic, which is a style inscribed in a time, a finished style.
The latter, on the other hand, can be reborn and translate the
same inspiration into new forms. The baroque would thus be
a "cultural style," partly because beyond art properly speaking, one can find it in literature, in manners, in daily existence,
and partly because, like the phoenix, it can be reborn from its
ashes and, under close or similar forms, know a new vitality.

Without pushing the comparison further, but passing it to
writers who are specialists in the matter, I remind the reader
that the metaphor of the baroque well defines the essential
characteristics of the aesthetic *style*—very precisely in its
postmodern expression.[24] On the one hand, this allows us to
stress the plurality of elements within the social globality, and
on the other hand, one can see how these elements manage to
enter into synergy and lead to a new form of equilibrium,
even if the latter is changing, dynamic, aleatory, and always
unstable. For our purpose, such a comparison allows us
above all to integrate, as structuring elements, hedonism and
the pleasure of being-togetherness. These may take very different forms; whether in sport, music, religion, tourism, leisure, or consumption, they nevertheless refer back to a culture that, like it or not, seems to assert itself with force at the
century's end. Denial no longer suffices, moralist vituperation
is useless, and since the movement is deep and especially
rooted in daily life, it is best to appreciate its positive aspects.

Style and Daily Life

Happiness, "this new idea," has become eminently suspect.
And for good cause, since it is so true that bourgeoisist mo-

dernity had confined it to a restricted space, that of the private, that of the tiny individual sphere that had a stale odor about it. But there could be another conception of happiness, one that envisages it as a social force, which means that individual happiness has dignity only if it is obtained within the framework of a collective happiness. Such a perspective puts the accent on the organic aspect of things, that is to say, on the fact that the intimate, lived experience has as much importance as that which is reputedly noble or serious (for example, the economic and political) in the constitution of social life. In fact, to take up Stendhal's celebrated phrase, "the pursuit of happiness" can also be lived in the quotidian, and hence, as with everything that bears this mark, have an essentially collective dimension.

One cannot insist strongly enough on the nobility of daily life. One could say it is starting from the "ordinary" that knowledge of the social develops. It behooves us to insist on this point since, on the one hand, it concerns a domain that as a blind spot was until now strangely ignored by intellectuals, and on the other, this quotidian seems to be one of the important characteristics of the aesthetic style that preoccupies us here. This can be observed in different ways. After having been long discredited, expressions such as "daily life" or "the mundane" seem to have become sorts of deus ex machina that one uses, on occasion, when one does not really know what to say. Politicians, decision makers, journalists, and even sociologists who are trying to recycle themselves—many are the users, more or less well intentioned, of what appears to them a fashionable "concept."

Let us leave these versatile people without convictions to their illusions; tomorrow they will turn to other, more marketable "concepts." To the contrary, we may discover that this fashion is an interesting index of what is a popular preoccupation, because the quotidian is not a concept with which one may play more or less as one likes in the ivory tower of intellectual coteries. It is a *style* in the sense that I have given the term, that is to say, something encompassing, ambient, that is cause and effect, at a given moment, of social relations as a whole. To put it another way, the mood of the times, life without quality, recognizes itself in the concrete and does so because this concrete is lived as a totality. Hermann Broch even speaks of "the universal daily life of an epoch," daily life in its infinite facets, by which the spirit of an epoch expresses itself.[25]

In taking up the oft-mentioned distinction between culture, as a founding moment, and civilization, as a fading of this same culture, we may recall that culture is perceived and experienced as a concrete totality. All facets of existence are included in it on the same level. There is no hierarchy among these facets and, moreover, there is no separation or break between them, as was the case for modernity. The stress on the quotidian as a concrete globality, that which Walter Benjamin called "the most extreme concrete," could thus lead us to say that we are witnessing a culture at birth—another way of speaking of the style of an epoch.

To follow up on this, we may remember that style can be considered, *stricto sensu,* as an "incarnation," or else as the concrete projection of all those emotional attitudes, those ways of thinking and acting, in short, of all the relations with the other by which a culture is defined. In this respect, we will speak of a worldview, but meanwhile bearing in mind that it is most often nonconscious, nonperceived (precisely) as a view: it is, on the other hand, widely experienced in everyday life. The term *habitus* (Oswald Spengler and Marcel Mauss) takes good account of these ways of being, living, and thinking that are activated in each individual and thereby constitute the body social. Having made this more precise, I intend to underline that there is a constant reversibility between the particular, what each one of us thinks and does, and, if not the universal, then at least the most widespread ways of thinking and acting. I would not say that singularity does not exist, but that it is exceedingly rare, and especially insignificant for the sociologist. In illustration of this thesis, it suffices to refer to the paradox of fashion—conceived, by its very principle, in order to distinguish oneself from others, but which logically can only spread, and hence end, very quickly, in indistinction.

By caricaturing my words, one could say that daily life is a good revelation of the style of an epoch, since it brings out the way in which existence is determined by the sense of the collective. By this I mean determination in the logical and etymological sense of *determinatio*. Logically, that which limits. Etymologically, that which stakes out, encloses (a field), but also that which gives life, permits there to be a culture in opposition to the undetermined of the desert. Because of these constraints, the uses and customs of the habitus, all individual life is limited. But at the same time, it is this very limitation that permits existence. In this sense daily life is that "subterranean centrality," that nodal point, to which one can pay no attention, that one can forget or deny, but that no less for all that constitutes the terrain on which all individual life will grow.

A phrase of Simmel's summarizes the idea: "All these banal and exterior events are in the end linked by structural wires that lead to final options bearing on the meaning and style of life."[26] This clearly accentuates the reticular system that is daily life—a subtle and complex network in which each element, object, subject, anodyne situation, significant event, thought, action, relationship, and so forth is worth only as much as it is related to the whole and makes sense only in and through globality. This is what is perceived, in a more or less conscious manner, in the contemporary valorization of the quotidian. One feels oneself in correspondence with others; one participates, along with others, in a more vast ensemble. All the different crowd-gatherings, collective emotions, festive effervescences, tribal attractions, and other sartorial, gestural, and linguistic fashions merely underline, on a daily basis, the pregnant import of a lifestyle that no one can escape. Contagion is the order of the day. *Virus* is certainly one of the key words of the moment. It announces a confusion of manners, ways of being and thinking that make each and every one an element of a general gregariousness. One can be offended by this or, on the contrary, valorize it as being the return of the communitarian ideal—it all depends. In any case, from the descriptive point of view that is mine here, it is necessary to take into account such a process and to recognize that it finds its origin and its purpose in this home *(foyer)* that is the quotidian, which, by this fact, is summoned to recover its titles of nobility.

The place occupied by the quotidian in the style of the epoch possesses essentially two aspects: on the one hand, it cannot be reduced to the simple instrumental reason of utilitarianism, and on the other, it puts an end to compartmentalization and the separation that were imposed during modernity. Of course, these two aspects are linked to each other; there is a constant reversibility between them. In a premonitory fashion, one finds this in the "philosophy of life" *(Lebensphilosophie)* proper to German romanticism, or again in what was experienced in the fin de siècle Vienna that was, as has often been pointed out, a laboratory of postmodernity.

As an example, one might refer to Robert Musil's *Man without Qualities,* whose main character, Ulrich, stands up against an instrumental rationality resting on the objective and univocal analysis of reality. To designate this rationality, one that stresses general laws and concepts, Musil uses the neologism "the ratioïd." He also shows that general laws and the eternal truths issuing from this rationality lead to a fragmented and separated reality . . . in a word, to an abstract one.

This is why Musil later challenges it with another conception of rationality, one more open and enlarged, that integrates the particular, the concrete aspect of existence, the aleatory. This results in the opposition between overarching morality of the law pronounced a priori and the ethical search for a just life based on experience, in which sentiment has a nonnegligible share.[27] Musil's critique of "the ratioïd" results, then, in privileging the individual lived experience, but a lived that is inscribed in an ensemble, which is only worth something because it participates in a whole. To do this, the image, the analogy, and everything that had been evacuated by rationalism now are given a prime position, precisely because they break the univocalism of interpretation, and, on the one hand, they account for the polysemy of lived experience, yet, on the other, they are cause and effect of a sociality that is not cut up into slices and in which being-togetherness, as the expression suggests, is lived in common.

It so happens that the romantic "philosophy of life," or even what was lived and described in the laboratory of fin de siècle Vienna, finds in our day an evident actuality. The lived, as a globality, is more and more the order of the day. And in contrast to an economy of existence, it is lifestyle that tends to predominate—a lifestyle, as I have said, that is hedonistic, aesthetic, and mystical. It is a lifestyle that stresses the play of appearances and the immaterial aspects of existence—in a paradoxical way, through the manipulation of images or even through the frantic consumption of objects. In each of these cases, it is no longer activism, production, or work that prevails, with the social consequences we know about, but indeed a will to live *(vouloir-vivre)* that we must here under-

stand in its strictest meaning. The "transfiguration of the political" clearly marks this evolution: one intends less to "act"
on the social, to affect society, than to take from it all the well-
being one can and to best enjoy this well-being. Political dis-
engagement, the derision of which politics is the object, is not
a transitory epiphenomenon. It is the profound mark of a refusal of the distant, a distrust of postponing enjoyment ("wait
until it is on sale"), and other forms of projects that put off
until the next day the possibility of living better. It is in the de-
pression of the political that the rage for the present finds its
niche, the concern for the here and now—what I have called
the ethic of the present instant.

In short, there is in this lifestyle an acquiescence to existence such as it is, an acquiescence that is by no means blind
toward all the dangers and dysfunctions of the moment. It is
certain that unemployment, violence, economic constraints,
the threats of moralism, and other forms of alienation are felt
as so many impositions that bridle, alter, or hamper a flour-
ishing social and individual life. But all that does not prevent
one from being engaged in experiencing, at best, what one
can enjoy. One could even say that, faced with these constraints, there is a frenzy to enjoy, a carpe diem, a surfeit of social energy that no longer is carried over into the future, but
invests itself in the present. Acquiescence to life is all the more
strong when it is most menaced. Such a relativist position—
let us enjoy to the maximum what we can—is the sign of a
tragic conception of existence; tragic since, in contrast to the
dramatic conception of bourgeoisism, trying to overtake dia-
lectically the contradictions, it accommodates itelf to them
and makes a virtue out of weakness. In other words, such a
conception makes of the tragic a force that, in a stoical manner, does not intend to act on that over which it has no control, but brings its creation to bear on that which is "at

hand," the quotidian, domestic, nearby—all things on the basis of which one can make of existence a veritable work of art.

There is nothing optimistic in this attitude, any more than there is of the catastrophic. And here we should refuse, as irrelevant, the orthodox sociology, somewhat blinded, of those who think they can continue to manage the social in a rational manner, just as much as we should refuse the metasociology, perhaps more lucid but no less blinded by all the defunct social values, that is incapable of appreciating the vitality, the force of creation in the tragic relativism at issue. If we take a paroxysmal example, we could say that the very real threat of an atomic catastrophe could be experienced "as a characteristic element of this new way of living our experience," as the philosopher Gianni Vattimo remarks,[28] which underlines my point. This threat could be considered the condensed form of all the social impositions of which I have spoken. It is the symbol of that over which one has no control, and it represents the tragic par excellence. Despite all that, however, or rather because of all that, a new communal experience is born that, "knowing," not necessarily in a conscious way, that the worst is always certain thus no longer situates itself in relation to a History to be mastered, but in relation to a present that is to be managed, that one should enjoy one way or another.

To say yes to life anyway: this is the challenge thrown down by postmodern sociality; this is also the epistemological stake with which we are confronted. In this focus on the quotidian, there is a sort of conservation of self, as of the species. It is a matter of a "knowledge" that is incorporated, and almost conscious, that "knows" that in the niche of the domestic one can, at best, resist the different impositions of established institutions and powers.

As we can see, there is in this lifestyle, no matter how aesthetic and mythic it is, an alternative attitude to the political. It is no longer the myth of emancipation, developed over the course of modernity, that prevails—the myth at the origin of the democratic ideal—but another way of being-togetherness in which consensus, close to its etymology *(cum sensualis)* is more affective and emotional than rational. The culture of sentiment that ensues from this is no less effective. Whether through gentleness, indifference, or abstention, the sociality in question knows how to make itself heard. Even its silence is eloquent, and at the present time it gives cold sweats to diverse politicians, trade unionists, and administrators who no longer know where to turn, "which saint to honor," since the masses are so unfathomable, versatile, and subject to variation. This tells us how much credit we should grant to various journalistic polls or statistical studies by the so-called social "sciences"!

In fact, the style of daily life is crisscrossed by the aleatory that is the very property of the aesthetic, that of communal emotion, which can bring itself to bear on some object, then on some other; it can be stirred by one idea, then by another, quite opposite, one; it can be fired by some hero, guru, or star of politics, music, or sports, and abandon that star, just like that. Communal emotion is called upon to remind us that power is indeed fragile—sic transit gloria mundi—faced with the persistence of strength. Periodically this strength resumes importance and tends to marginalize power. Here I am not going to develop this power-versus-strength dialectic. It suffices to suggest that the aesthetic style, the force of the quotidian, the gentle resistance that this induces—all is certainly the expression of the reinvestment of social strength, that "invisible collective force" of which Bakunin spoke and that sometimes moves life in society in an irresistible way. Thus one sees that the notion of style is not simply a topic of conversation for dinners in town: it is at the heart of what is taking shape in this nascent postmodernity.

By way of a historical example, we may recall that certain societies, and not the minor ones, placed the accent on such a way of being. I am thinking in particular of ancient Greece, which made the culture of the self the pivot of city organization. Not being an expert in the subject, I only offer a metaphoric reference, intended to illuminate the present time. This "care for the self," as Foucault said, was by no means synonymous with a withdrawal into oneself, but, on the contrary, worked largely to influence relations with others: conjugal life, civic activities, economic relations, and even the relation with nature. Thus, the subject of pleasure or the search for hedonism was an original social posture, a specific manner of behaving in relation to the natural environment and the social environment; in short, it determined a "stylistic of existence."

From such a perspective, it is indeed the daily life of the subject that is determining the social life as a whole. Even dreams play a part, one that is not negligible in moral experience. In his analysis of Artemidorus and his book on dreams, Foucault shows the close relation that exists between the sexual conduct of a subject and his familial, social, and economic existence. Thus, an assessment of a particular sexual conduct is not made in itself, abstractly, but by reference to other domains of social life. He calls this relation, this reversibility, the "style of activity" of the subject.[29] The expression is felicitous in that it underlines the fact that sexual life, this quotidian par excellence, is not only a permanent part of social life, but even gives it its particular style.

This style, it is important to stress, owes nothing to an overarching and general law or to a persnickety code that "lays down the law," functioning on the logic of "the duty of being," in short, according to a principle engendering frustration. Rather, this style relies on a "savoir faire" that knows, according to the incorporated knowledge to which I have al-

luded, that there is an individual and social equilibrium to be
preserved and that acts as a consequence of this. It is what
Foucault names a "stylization of the attitude and an aesthetisization of existence."[30] I would add that as a function of this
coenesthetic sense, that is, as a function of an equilibrium
knowingly integrating both function and dysfunction, everything is allowed, nothing is forbidden, since everything, including the anomic, is integrated in proportion, as one could
craftily say. There is no transgression, which is a notion of
Christian origin, but rather a sort of innocence, that can be
perverse, in which "everything is good": amorous camarade-
rie, love of boys, troilism, bisexuality, "group sex"—everything enters into a stylization that makes of the quotidian an
art, for which each and every one is responsible in the general
framework of the collective equilibrium. One finds here "the
just life" that was in question and that belongs to an ethic
coming from below, in opposition to a morality imposed from
above.

What one should retain from this analysis is that quotidian
style may, in certain epochs, give form and figure to the whole
of society. It does not decree how one should behave and why
it is necessary to do or not to do this or that, but is content to
foster, or just to tolerate, the use of pleasures, whatever they
are, from the most anodyne to the most perverse, as a condition of possibility of a being-togetherness in equilibrium. This
would be like a small-scale utopia, knowing that the flowering of each person, at the very heart of the quotidian, can only
valorize the collective well-being. It would seem, without
this appearing as an explicit claim, that it is this flowering
and, as a result of it, this well-being that perhaps now come
back into the agenda. All juvenile practices move in this direction, and the "style of activity" that they propel among the
young is oriented toward a concern for authenticity, a search

for creation, and this as much at the level of work properly speaking as in their life in general. We should bear this in mind, if only to relativize the ominous opinion in some quarters that says that from the moment that certain values cease to exist, there are no more values at all.

In fact, as the principal value of productive ideology, to wit, work for work's sake, tends to become saturated, one can see another type of value moving into place, with still somewhat nebulous outlines, but allying creation and pleasure. It is thus that one could interpret everything that smacks of enterprise culture: the importance of affective interactions in the context of work, the constitution of teams as a function of nonrational criteria, and the creation of cooperatives, of associations of human scale, in which the relational factor plays a nonnegligible role. In all these cases, we can say that the aesthetic style of the quotidian contaminates a domain that until then was subject to the purely economic reality principle, and to a rational organization of which Taylorism was the ultimate expression. The search for the qualitative—a preoccupation of the contemporary quotidian in urbanism, leisure, neighborhoods—does not leave untouched the realm of production and services, and indeed highlights the spirit, the aesthetic and immaterial dimension, that will serve as a matrix for social life.

Writing a hermeneutic analysis of Proust, the Italian philosopher Maurizio Ferraris states that properly a text "prima di descrivere una realtà già data, trasmette e stilizza forme di vita" (before describing an already given reality, transmits and stylizes forms of life).[31] From this perspective, each text is an act of shaping. Here is a particularly pertinent remark about the specific ambience exuded by Proust's work, in which what prevails is less the historical framework than the "climatic" variations in which the protagonists of the novel

bathe and that make them become what they are. It is certain
*that, just as I have stated for Musil's Man without Qualities,
Remembrance of Things Past* is in many respects a work that
heralds postmodernity. And, in this sense, what is said of the
literary text may be extrapolated to the "text" of daily life,
that of immediate and banal life, in which what matters is less
the content, the doing, the base, than savoir faire, appearance, and form—whose importance in daily interactions we
know. This savoir faire will of course include the rules of po-
liteness, the diverse rituals of sociability, the codes of behavior
in society. One also finds it in what constitutes business relations, in a way of expounding theories, in academic ideas,
journalistic analyses, or quite simply in bureaucratic and institutional relations, in which what is important, more than
the basis, is to know how to "present" a case well. One could
at leisure extend the list of situations that are worth something only because they are stylizations of forms of life.

After having given previously an illustration taken from the
ancient world, I will give another that belongs to contemporary society, that of Japan. We know the role played there by
kata, which can be rendered by the notion of form or style.
Kata consists of "learning through the body." Thus are ac-
quired a certain number of practices that make life in society
possible—in addition, kata has been presented as that which
gave "armatures to collective conducts"—just as much in the
framework of spirituality (hence Zen) as in what concerns
daily acts (the tea ceremony, flower arranging). Of course,
each of these "arts" gives rise to specific ceremonies, to particular moments, but they are equally diffused onto all the occasions of daily life, imprinted with a ritualization that does
not fail to strike the foreign observer. It is no less certain that
Western influence tends to make of these "forms" something
rather abstract, and Philippe Pons, an excellent connoisseur

of Japanese life, has many times insisted on the mercantile aspect that kata takes these days.[32]

The fact that "stylism," induced by the notion of kata, deeply impregnates the whole of Japanese social life would have a merely ethnological interest if one did not know the importance of the role Japan plays at this century's end. And for my part, I consider that the competitiveness of the Japanese economy, its aggressiveness in the economic war, the extraordinary dynamism of its businesses, the stability of its currency—all these rest, in part, on the potentialities of kata (form, style) that have constituted a collective sensibility and that are constantly engaged in mobilizing it. The initiation made by kata teaches the student to accord with the "rhythm of the breathing of the universe," quite an Oriental formula, difficult to comprehend for a Cartesian mind, but one that finds concrete expression in the martial arts. In truth, it does not matter how you theorize what is above all a practice, a set of practices, that can be compared to that "style of activity" of which Foucault spoke in relation to the apprenticeship of young Greeks. What is important is the existence of a collective sensibility that, learned and lived on a daily basis, then has the effects we know of in professional, social, and religious life.

Style and Communication

As paradoxical as it might appear, the "network" of the image—constituted by style, form, and the play of appearances—in this nascent postmodernity gives a singular force to the communitarian ideal. We have trouble admitting this, since our modes of analysis are very much fashioned by democratic individualism, and so everything that does not lend itself to this schema is, a priori, suspect. It is true that in many respects the communitarian resurgence can be worrisome. Current events, with their cries and furies, are there to remind us of the dangers inherent in religious, ethnic, or linguistic communitarianism. We need to be conscious of this problem. The diverse daily solidarities, the multiplicity of friendly, cultural, sexual, and sport groupings are there to prove it. However it happens to be, paroxysmally or mundanely, amid horror or mellowness, this new being-togetherness is there, well and truly present. And nothing is accomplished by denying it, or by doubting its existence and scope, at the risk of brutal awakenings when we are regularly reminded of its manifestations.

Hence, it is around an image, as a function of a style, that this being-togetherness takes form, *stricto sensu*. This merits attention, in particular because it explodes the logic of identity that had prevailed throughout modernity. I have already shown that unique identity—sexual, professional, or ideological identity—has given way to a series of successive identifications. I will not return to this problem again. In fact, one could show that this slippage is taking effect, precisely, thanks to the prevalence of the world of the image, and that in style it finds its ultimate expression. The contraction within identification, which is of recent origin (the Cartesian cogito is a good reference point here), took effect under the impulse of a rationalist conception of the individual and of society. Here is the famous "disenchantment with the world," whose scope Max Weber well demonstrated. This has engendered both the withdrawal into the self and a contractual attitude, of which the different classes, strata, and other socioprofessional categories are the social expressions.

Faced with this, postmodern reenchantment, by means of the image, myth, and allegory, gives rise to an aesthetic that essentially has an aggregative function: hence the accent

placed on notions like magic, charm, vision, appearance—
that characterize contemporary style and that are cause and
effect, in everyday life, of that "linking" that does not fail to
astonish social observers. At the turn of the past century, in
Art from a Sociological Viewpoint, Jean-Marie Guyau judi-
ciously showed how sociology played "a considerable role in
the increasing penetrability of consciousness." To designate
the kind of sympathy, in its strongest sense, to which this gave
rise, he even spoke of a "realized society of souls."[33] It is a
suggestive expression that well brings out the erotic communication emanating from the aesthetic.

These days one could extrapolate Guyau's thesis and show
that it is life as a whole that has become a work of art. In effect, numerous are the situations that engender this "increasing penetrability of awareness." Emotion cannot be reduced
to the single sphere of the private, but is lived collectively, to
an ever greater extent. One could even speak of an affective
ambience in which pains and pleasures are experienced in
common. It suffices to mention the role played by television
during catastrophes, wars, or other bloody events in order to
be convinced of this. It is the same with great national or international commemorations, royal weddings, or society
events involving musical "stars" or celebrities of all kinds. Finally, one finds this ambience in the staging *(mise-en-scène)* of
the crowds assembled for diverse sporting, musical, religious,
or political events. In each of these cases, television permits
participants to "vibrate" together. One cries, laughs, or
stamps one's feet in unison, and thus, without actually being
in the presence of each other, a kind of communion is created
whose social effects are still to be measured.

What has just been said about television is even more obvious with respect to all the festive, ludic, or quite simply banal
occasions that punctuate everyday life. There is a mysterious

link that unites the diverse protagonists of these gatherings. Even if it is provisional and aleatory, the "society of souls" is regularly realized, and any occasion serves for doing so. This is evident in the multiplicity of parties or festivals of a cultural character, but one also finds it in commercial fairs and in political meetings or demonstrations. Even scientific congresses and colloquia are not immune to such frivolity. In each case, there is a gregarious impulse, as it were, that pushes one to seek out others, to touch them, and incites one to get lost in the mass as if in a more vast entity where one can express, by contagion, that which enclosure within identity does not permit. The individual, in losing himself, in expending herself in such a "society of souls," knows or feels that he or she is gaining a "boost of existence," that of participating in a community that turns his or her loss into a net profit.

In opposition to the mechanical and purely rational organization of classicism, we know that art historians attributed this tactile impulse to the baroque. The metaphor is interesting in that it brings out the fact that there is an organic order within fusion, even within confusion. That is to say, everything and everyone has a place there—a place that without being identical or egalitarian, and in many respects even being inscribed in a sort of hierarchy, does not fail to render each thing indispensable to the whole. Akin to the baroque, there is in postmodern style an organic necessity. The particular and individual are effaced in order to cede to the "type" or the typical to which one is aggregated, but which, at the same time, gives life. By participating, in the mystical sense of the term, in some musical, sports, religious, or political "type," by copying or even sometimes mimicking a political figure, a singer, or a guru who best exemplifies this "type," each is integrated into an ensemble that allows it both to live and to enter into correspondence with others. From such a perspective, the autonomy of the subject as master and lord of itself no longer holds. Similarly, its erstwhile strong identity is fissured in many places. In contrast, an identification (or identifications) emerges that makes my ego a heteronomous being, someone who only exists through and thanks to the other. For better or worse, a new social order is thereby defined.

It is a question of a communicational order, symbolic in the strongest sense of the word, an order that, after the parenthesis of modernity founded on the *principium individuationis,* once again finds the *principium relationis* of traditional or primitive societies. Such a putting-into-relation is multiform, and it touches many domains of social life: religious, cultural, political, social. It has something of the archaic in the sense that it reinvests this primary impulse that causes the search for a communitarian space in which the individual is worth something only as a function of the group into which he or she is inserted. It is precisely this that allows us to speak of tribalism.

We should recall that this is a matter of a phenomenon that has already existed in traditional societies. Let us not forget, either, that what one calls postmodern is, in part, the reprise of premodern elements that are now utilized and lived in a different manner. Finally, we should signal that during the modern period one finds more-or-less important "traces" of the feeling of belonging from which the communitarian ideal is shaped. Thus, what has been called "class consciousness" or "national consciousness," in addition to their rational justifications, rests in large part on a form of collective narcissism made up of shared emotions, sentiments, and passions. A number of testimonies about and research into the Communist Party, or more recently, the National Front, to take only the paroxysmal examples, bring out clearly the role and the place of affect in their internal organizations. In the sense given by Pareto to this term, the sentiment of belonging, the impulse toward aggregation, is truly a "residue" that, with greater or lesser force, is always at work in any life or society.

It is by bearing this in mind that one can understand how the contemporary aesthetic finds a form of realization in the communicational style, which signifies that social life is only a series of "copresences"—or, to put it in a more poetic manner by borrowing Rimbaud's expression, "I is another." Certainly it is possible to interpret this expression in different ways, but essentially it reminds us that the individual, far from being an isolated atom, can only exist and grow by assuming a role in an ambience of communion.[34] This allows each and every one to express and to live the multiple potentialities of its being.

We are far from the intangible function assumed by the individual within the framework of instrumental functionality proper to modernity. A role has something more aleatory and more uncertain about it. But of course there is also something more ludic, even more oneiric. One dreams one's life, or one's lives, and thus one is integrated into the more global imaginary of the community. More precisely, role games, with their oneiric charge, are both cause and effect of this communitarian imaginary. It suffices, in this respect, to think of juvenile attitudes toward the sexual economy, the relation to work or to ideologies, to measure the impact of this role playing. We often hear people deplore the loss of moral sense, or the multiplicity of amorous relations, ideological unpredictability, or versatility, and the lack of continuity in professional activity—all of which our societies are supposedly victims of. In each case, what is going on is quite simply the passage from one role to another, what I have called a series of "successive sincerities." One gives oneself utterly, totally, to a professional activity, sometimes to an ideology or to an amorous relation. But the authenticity at work in this "gift" is only momentary, and when it is saturated one plays another role, which one assumes with no less authenticity.

It is in this sense that the communicational style breaks with the logic of identity, with the principle of individuation. Francis Jacques expresses it in his own way: the other is "structurally present within the self."[35] And in effect one must begin with the alterity that is at the core of the "I" ("I is another") in order to understand postmodern sociality. Here we find again the thematic of the Dionysiac. Dionysus, the god "of a hundred faces," the god of versatility, of play, of the tragic and the loss of the self, casts his shadow over our societies. It is no longer the presence of a celestial Apollo, luminous and rational, who prevails, but rather that of a more earthly figure, in whom obscurity and ambivalence have their place. With Dionysus it is the myth of ambiguity that is reborn. The role of alterity at the heart of the "I" and, in consequence, at the heart of the social as a whole, should be understood in this way. It is this ambiguity, constitutive of contemporary modernity, that characterizes the style of our era and that may invite us to choose a communicational approach to subjectivity.

In other words, the fusional "we" takes on importance anew, as a concatenation of "we's," through which twirls each person (persona), multiple in itself. I must insist—if not on the novelty, since there are few new things under the sun— then on the return of such a thematic, that of the communitarian ideal. It includes the "concrete experience of standing in a relationship to others, a relationship maintained by communication—that is, a philosophy conceived from a directly relational point of view."[36] The relational principle puts into play, in the strong sense of the word, someone who, either by verbal communication or by nonverbal communication, is always in interaction with the other at the heart of oneself, or with others at the heart of the social. There is in such a perspective something qualitatively different, something that may appear strange and unaccustomed to a way of thinking forged around the principle of individuation in order to analyze modern individualism. This does not make it any less true that egocentric ideology no longer holds sway as soon as, empirically, communitarian fusions and communicational relations prevail.

Let us not be mistaken: this communitarian ideal may be, in many respects, illusory. This communication may be equally empty of meaning. The problem is not there. We do not have to say "ought-to-be," or bring a value judgment to bear, but above all to report what is the case—since, to take up an expression of Van Gogh's, "one must bravely believe that what is, is." What exists contemporarily is indeed the profusion of aggregations and communitarian and communicational myths. And that is enough.

So it matters little that the content of the communication attains its degree zero. It is enough that one believes in it, in order for it to be pertinent for the social observer—even more so since we are too accustomed to judge the content as a function of consciousness, of instrumental reason, or of other purposes. There might be a communication that had as its sole objective to "touch" the other, to simply be in contact, to participate together in a form of gregariousness. This is the communication of sport, of music, of consumption, or else that banal communication of the daily or weekly stroll through the urban spaces designed for this effect. This "tactile" communication is also a form of address: we speak to each other by touching. This may bring a smile to our Cartesian and moralizing minds. And yet the erotic induced by such communication is also part of social being-togetherness, and numerous are the societies that were constituted on the basis of it. It happens that now, with the media aiding and abetting it (and we tend to agree in the opinion that they represent, in effect, the degree zero of content), this "tactile" communication takes on an unsuspected scope and hence merits more ample attention.

When I say "tactile" communication, I am thinking of an encompassing ambience that tends to a kind of uniformity that is equally well observed in ways of thinking as in ways of being, or, quite simply, in sartorial or gestural appearances. In this respect, one could speak of a becoming fashion of the world. But we should not understand such a process in a univocal way. In fact, this fashion is in no way unique. Contrary to how it has been analyzed by critical theory over the past decades, fashion is not concocted, abstractly, by a few dispensaries representing the interests of capital or else, according to a slightly antiquated formula, by the "Ideological State Apparatuses." In fact, this fashion is inscribed in a process of reversibility, and only crystallizes a diffuse expectation at the heart of basic sociality. And as much as with advertising, musical infatuations, or even political, ideological, or religious hits, what "works" well is above all that which is lived and integrated by the largest number. In this sense the media, and television in particular, merely play the role of an echo sending back to the masses the images they have of themselves: they are only the mirror of the different collective narcissisms to which I referred.

One must remember that, contrary to different kinds of interpretations, Narcissus does not drown himself by wanting to rejoin his image with which he has fallen in love. In falling into the pool, he loses himself in the cosmos symbolized by this pool. One could say, metaphorically, that it is the same with the televisual screen: the narcissism of the group drowns itself in it, recognizing its own image, but, by these means, it is social globality with which one communes. Here lies the interlocution at issue; there is not really just one or a few enunciators, and what counts is the interlocutive relation. It is a form of "we say." This means that there is not a preestablished meaning, or that televisual discourse has no precise meaning, or that there is no meaning at all, but rather that it is just a "pooling in common of the meanings" lived by the largest number. One could, in this respect, refer to the etymology of the term *discourse:* discurrere, meaning to run in several directions,[37] and to do so in a disorganized, chaotic, and aleatory manner. The discourse of the media, in the likeness of a social that no longer has precise orientations or that no longer believes in tales of overarching reference, has no preestablished purposes, but instead haphazardly expresses the passions, affects, and sentiments lived day to day in immediate existence.

Looking at it more closely, there is nothing catastrophic in such a perspective, and it only accentuates the importance of the "we," the prevalence of a "being-togetherness" that has no other purpose than being together. This is another way of describing an aesthetic style that privileges the fact of feeling in common, and so of recognizing oneself in the means, meaning in the media that express such a common emotion. Thereby postmodernity foresakes a logic of representation in order to enter into a logic of perception. So we are concerned with a style of commutability in general that is no longer egocentric but rather is situated in a "common interlocutory context."[38] Popular wisdom says that everything is just a matter of context, which thereby aligns it with the sharp analyses of sensible observers like Abraham Moles, for whom "to communicate is to use what one has in common." Such a contextualization is most pertinent for understanding what I have called the degree zero of content, and by the same token the vanity of intellectual analyses that seek meaning (understood as rational) where it does not exist. It is a property of context precisely, that there is no unique case; each thing depends on the angle of attack from which it is approached. The context is essentially multicausal, polysemic, and plural, and it favors the perception of things en masse, and so it allows us to understand the masses as well as the different movements that animate them.

It is also contextualization that allows us to grasp the different contagions that regularly run away with the body social. They are disconcerting and in general leave social observers flabbergasted, since these people have difficulty thinking in terms of epidemiology. The principles of individuation and individualism, *terminus a quo et terminus ad quem* of modern philosophy and sociology, do not favor the apprehension of mass movements. Nevertheless, it is indeed collective trances that are at work in all the effervescent or banal crowd gatherings that punctuate everyday life. And with an immutable ritual, television offers these effervescences to a blissful crowd who feast their eyes on them. According to a rehearsed liturgy, newscasts span the day, and in between, game shows, series, variety and "reality" shows, magazine items on major sports, "cultural," political, or high-society events all demonstrate the diverse deliriums of the era. The summit is attained with the broadcast of football matches, the Olympic Games and various world trophies in which agglutination in front of, or rather being glued to, the TV set should be analyzed in terms of magic participation and may be compared to the Aboriginal corroboree festivals described by Durkheim; thanks to them, according to his phrase, the community "comforts the sentiment it has of itself."[39] After the fashion of "manna" for primitive tribes, from the television object emanates an immaterial force that assures the cohesion of postmodern tribes.

In this sense we could say that the aesthetic style makes use of different means of communication in order to comfort a

being-togetherness, which no longer pretends to be conceptual but rather, essentially, affective. Thus the Roman exigency of *panem et circenses* is replayed, and since in advanced
societies bread is almost guaranteed, it is circus games that
are needed. And even in societies where "bread," here understood in a metaphoric way, comes to be lacking, the object
television is always present. The profusion of antennae in the
various slums, favelas, and pueblos of the entire world is, in
this respect, the instructive illustration of the need to vibrate
in unison and to participate, even if that participation is only
faint, in a communitarian ensemble. Without mentioning
Dallas and its renowned success, a fine study of the Brazilian
telenovelas has clearly shown that at the precise hour the serial is broadcast, practically the entire country seems to stop,
so concerned is it to participate in a sort of sacramental
union, a profane Eucharist. My remarks are certainly exag-
gerated, but they bring out the necessity of an epidemiological
analysis. Like a virus, the affective contagion spreads, and the
success of the media is directly, and uniquely, tied to their capacity to diffuse a virus that is already inside the body social.

Regarding what he calls "neo-TV," Umberto Eco too reveals the absence of content, this deconceptualization: "It
speaks less and less of the exterior world . . . it speaks of itself
and of the context it is establishing with its audience."[40] The
external world, as a matter of fact, can be interpreted as that
distant thing no one cares about. On the other hand, what is
privileged are contact and interactivity, which seem to be the
tendency of the television of tomorrow—an interactivity that
makes a link and favors communion, even if the latter rests on
a void. This is what led people to say that the profusion of
communication is the symptom of the absence of communication—which is Jean Baudrillard's analysis, for example. It is a
correct appreciation, on condition that by the absence of

communication one means, necssarily, a communication having a content or delivering a precise message, but it is erroneous if one recognizes that there could exist a communication that, in all senses of the word, is used to touch the other, to favor contact with the other, either directly or indirectly. It seems that it may be this type of communication that prevails these days.

A nonverbal communication, or rather communication for which meaning is completely secondary; a relativist communication that by its deconceptualization favors relation: Having exhausted the delights of theories full of meaning such as they have been gradually elaborated during modernity, having witnessed the bankruptcy of all the utopias oriented to the future, and conscious of the vanity of the rationalist project, it would seem that postmodern sociality feels the need for what the poet Rilke called "the first silence." This entails leaving the mind fallow and valorizing the lived for what it bears of the close at hand and the concrete—a lived experience that is somewhat materialist and traversed by the taste for the present and for shared pleasure, that knows how to be quiet about what may not, or cannot, be spoken of. In its philosophical sense, all this has the allure of honest cynicism. It also testifies to a lucidity without illusions, pertaining to the man without qualities. Finally, it allows us to measure the dynamism of the aesthetic style, spreading more and more, and serving as fertile ground for the nascent sociality.

II. THE IMAGINAL WORLD

The exterior is an interior raised to the power of mystery.
NOVALIS

The Fear of the Image

IT IS BY BEING ATTENTIVE to the "signs of the times," and knowing how to interpret all those current events, slightly chaotic, strongly emotionally charged, that constitute everyday life, that one could be in a position to appreciate the new lifestyle that surreptitiously is spreading by capillary action in the body social. This is how shared sentiment (another way of saying myth) is revived, a sentiment that tends to express itself in a more-or-less perverse way and that above all has nothing of the rational about it—or at the very least is difficult to integrate into the rationalist scheme that has prevailed during all of modernity. In short, we can say that the image, the symbolic, the imaginary, and imagination itself come back to the forefront and are brought to play a starring role. It is this ensemble that I propose calling, borrowing and slightly distorting a term of Gilbert Durand's or Henry Corbin's, an "imaginal" world.

In this respect, it is wise to specify that I do not intend to make a philosophical analysis of the imaginary, but rather to establish this simple realization: a recognition of the profusion, the role, and the pregnant import of the image in social life. And, before tackling this head-on, it is perhaps useful to come back, if only for a moment, to the mental attitude that tends to minimize, if not to deny, the role the image plays in social life.

It has tended to become banal to speak of iconoclasm, but we too often forget to seek, beyond commonplaces, its source. Gilbert Durand, notably, has shown that there exists an ancient and fundamental distrust within the Judeo-Christian tradition, and in the Semitic one more generally, of the image. Certainly one could find, throughout the three or four millennia that form this tradition, some notable exceptions. Struggles, wars, battles of ideas between iconophiles and iconoclasts have even marked various significant periods: the Old Testament and the problem of idols, Byzantium and its persecutions, the Reformation and the cult of saints—all of these prove abundantly that the debate was never facile. But we should stress that the *phenomenal* world, that is, the world of images, was never envisaged except as separated from God. Let us not forget that it issued from original sin and remains, by this fact, in a state of total impiety. To take up an expression from Christian theology, the "phenomenal world is only conceivable in a state of aversion in relation to God."[1]

The expression is strong and encapsulates the irrepressible separation, that is to say, the difference in nature, the qualitative difference that exists between perfection (God) and imperfection (the world). Later on, to put it in a cavalier manner, we will again encounter such a separation between healthy

reason, the seat of perfection, the germ of God in human nature, and the imagination, quickly assimilated to insanity,
that represents everything in man that goes back to animality,
to the infrahuman—in a word, to the subterranean and de-
monic world from which one must take one's distance or
which one must try to redeem.

In the same spirit, it is from this that moralism developed,
whose importance I have already shown, especially its astonishing endurance not only in the religious world but also in
the intellectual class and that of opinion makers. In effect,
there is a close link between the refusal of appearances and
fear of the image in its various forms, on the one hand, and
the horror of meanings, the fear of beauty, or even the hatred
of matter, on the other. Nietzsche's whole work, but especially
his *Genealogy of Morals,* is engaged in showing and founding
such a link. And we could say, following him, that the refusal
of life, the abstractive attitude, or other forms of resentment
all find their origin in this "state of aversion."

Thus this aversion between God and the phenomenal
world has become an aversion between man and himself. This
is a curious slippage that might appear paradoxical, since
thereby man attacks his essential part: his being of the world,
his being through and in the world. There is nothing surprising in this, since very often the refusal of life, and of what life
possesses of the noncontrollable and the disordered, leads to
this "hatred of self" of which we know only too well the
paroxysmal,[2] and somewhat pathological cases, but which, in
a more banal and somehow totally "normal" way, is quite
widespread in the intellectual world.

Aversion, hatred of self, and the refusal of life certainly do
not present themselves in their pure states. In fact, they advance wearing masks. For my part, I consider that the distrust
of images is one of these masks. One could certainly find mul-

tiple theological, and then philosophical, illustrations of such a distrust; psychology or sociology is not spared of it, either. It suffices to recall that mistrust rests essentially on the desire, somewhat utopian, for the good functioning of the human spirit, liberated of various obscurantisms or primitive aftereffects. The image is one of these, as I have already suggested for Descartes, but one could equally see it in Francis Bacon, whose influence, which we discover right up through Wittgenstein, is far from negligible. So in the *Novum Organum* (1620), there are whole passages on different idols—*idola tribus, idola specus, idola fori*—that trouble healthy knowledge and true judgment.[3] In fact, the idol is indeed a human production, but a minor production, even dangerous since it is rooted in that *"part maudite"* (damned part) (Georges Bataille), that *"instant obscur"* (dark moment) (Ernst Bloch) that pulls us toward the depths, brings us close to the animals or—which is no better—to the chthonic spirits, earthly and of redoubtable energy. It is Dionysus, that treelike divinity, emblem of the pleasures lived in the here and now, hence of the sensorial, who stands opposed to Apollo, the Uranus god, torchbearer of the celestial light, that of pure reason.

In effect, in contrast to the latter, the image or the phenomenon does not pretend to exactitude or verisimilitude. It is only a vector of contemplation, of communion with others. What we could call the iconic function has no validity in itself, but is essentially an evocation, or rather a support, for other things: the relation to God, to others, to nature. In short, the image is relative, in the sense that it does not pretend to the absolute and that it puts things into relation. It is this very relativism that renders it suspect, since it does not allow the certainty, the security engendered by dogma, or even the good abstract reasoning that does not embarrass itself with factual, sensory, or emotional contingencies or other "frivolous" situations with which daily existence is filled. As we know, pure reason follows the *via recta* of utility and efficiency. According to a well-known symbol, it is a two-edged sword that decides, that distinguishes and separates. This symbolism has been well analyzed by Gilbert Durand, who, in his *Anthropological Structures of the Imaginary,* speaks of "diacritical schemas" in which "the double-edged sword comes to reinforce the threat of the specter"; one could say that knowledge becomes or comforts power. It is exactly this that means that "the diurnal regime has become the guiding mentality of the West."[4] It is perhaps this that made for the force of the latter: the search for and direct acquisition of the Truth have made reason something useful and effective. We know the scientific, technological, and productivist upshot of such a mentality.

Completely otherwise is the somewhat lustful, meandering, and admittedly lazy approach of the iconic function. It is not engaged in saying what "ought to be," but is content with what is, or—which comes down to the same thing—with what could be. From this comes the fictional side that it tends to favor. One always has the impression that it tells stories more than it speaks History. It follows the meanderings of life, its seething, which makes it appear less serious to an intellectual attitude that easily confuses "meaning" and "purpose." Whereas reason has as its consequence a will acting in the wake of what it has decided, the iconic is instead a manner of accounting for the laissez-faire "let it be" attitude that is the property of all vitalism. In this sense the image *takes note of* a vital élan, an emotional aesthetic *(aisthesis)* in all its affects, whether refined, in bad taste, unbridled, kitschy, explosive, or conformist. It is indeed this "let it be" of the iconic function that renders it suspect to the "activist" ideology of the *homo faber* that, in various guises, has marked Western thought—as witness this observation, a classical summation by a great thinker of this century, Miguel de Unamuno: "Abandoned to itself, human reason leads to absolute phenomenalism, to nihilism."[5]

Such an assessment is by no means excessive. And the terms used are significant—*abandoned, phenomenalism,* and *nihilism* are all pejorative in Unamuno's writing; curious, too, is the gradation that shows that reason in this state of "abandon" is pulled toward the bottom, is denatured into its contrary, "phenomenalism," with the superficial and frivolous aspect that this term does not fail to conjure. Everything is said in a few words, everything that belongs to the order of appearance and the phenomenal is stigmatized. And only a reason that ought to be engaged in the search for the "numinous," and therefore ought to be defending what is essential, to wit God—only such a reason has a valid and worthy activity. Everything else is of the order of the diabolical endeavor that may be fascinating, seductive, and possess (as common sense has it) the "devil's charm," but therefore bears the mark of sin and should therefore arouse aversion.

In the guise of a friendly polemic, one could find this "moralist" sensibility even among thinkers who would seem to be impervious to it. Here I am thinking of Jean Baudrillard, who has tried both to analyze the "after the orgy" and to put some order into the multiplication of images. Thus, for him, the iconoclasts are not those who "destroy images, but . . . [those who] manufacture a profusion of images there *in which there is nothing to see.*" This leads to an "ultra or infra-aesthetic."[6]

The argument is not lacking in pertinence and, to take but one example, it is true that the development of television might justify such a perspective. I will return elsewhere to this particular problem, but for the moment I will merely indicate that this critique is too attached to the content of the image,

which of course requires discrimination in qualitative terms—
images full or empty of meaning—and in quantitative terms
—too many images killing the content. This perspective does
not see the vessel-like aspect of the image; in effect, like an
empty ensemble, the image is above all a vector of communion: it matters less for the message that it is supposed to
carry than for the emotion it conveys. In this sense the image
is thoroughly orgiastic, strictly speaking passionate *("orge")*,
or even aesthetic: whatever the content, it favors collective
feeling *("aisthesis")*.

But it is with difficulty that the sensuality of the image is
received by the intellectualism by which we are shaped. And
to conclude this rapid anthology of distrust, or aversion to
appearances, one might recall the whole critique of the spectacle, inaugurated with vigor and relevance by the Situationists in the 1960s and now widely diffused in different domains. The media, of course, but also politics, contemporary
thought, and religion—nothing escapes the hold of the spectacle. But here again, the moralist critique of the spectacle,
seemingly in the name of a purely rational real, seems somewhat inadequate. A paroxysmal example of such a position
is Giorgio Agamben's analysis, pushing to the limits the logic
of Guy Debord's *Society of the Spectacle,* showing precisely
that the spectacle "is nothing but the pure form of separation: when the real world is transformed into an image and
images become real."[7] We should ask ourselves about this
conception of the "real"—practical, constructed, rational,
and thinkable. It is quite a limited conception that, at the
least, leaves out the efficacy of the unreal: the symbolic,
imaginary, or mythic.

But what this critique especially does not allow us to see is
that, by a process of inversion, the image becomes a vector of
communion, and henceforth bypasses the "separation" that

was the key concept in the critique of the spectacle. In fact, in the wake of Western iconoclasm, radical contemporary thought had trouble integrating everything of the order of the nonconscious, the nonrational, or even what belongs to the vast domain of nonverbal communication. Following Wilfred Pareto and Max Weber, one could say that what is nonlogical is not illogical, or that what is nonrational is not irrational, but may have its own logic or rationality.

The image, the phenomenon, the appearance all belong to those things that, while not having a precise purpose or an "instrumental rationality," or perhaps because they have neither one nor the other, are in a position to express that "hyperrationality" of which the utopian Charles Fourier spoke, made up of dreams, the ludic, the oneiric and of fantasy, and which seems more pertinent for describing the real or the "hyperreal" that agitates social life. It is just this that one could call the "imaginal" world, which is like a matrix in which all the elements of earthly data interact, resonate in concert, or correspond to each other in multiple ways and in a constant reversibility. In this sense, one could say without paradox that the imaginal world, in a *realistic* manner, takes seriously each of these elements, whatever it is, and is therefore going to constitute the contemporary or postmodern reality.

One could even say that in evoking or invoking things for what they are, and without regard to what is beyond them or the Beyond, the image is close to this "real" that Western rationality would like to apprehend, act on, or explain with all its might. In fact, Elias Canetti has clearly shown that the dialectic, in its infinite process of mediations, overcoming of negations and contradictions, makes what it intends to grasp disappear. It is the same with the concept of the unconscious for psychoanalysis that goes on to transform everything into the signifier (of something else), which means that nothing exists in itself.[8] Now, the dialectic and the unconscious, as such, or under other similar names, are the fine points of Western thought, a kind of thought that, in a nutshell, aims at something other than what is, something other than what is seen, something other than what is there. And although it may well be banal, it is not useless to recall that phenomenology (and not "phenomenalism") takes seriously the thing in itself, whatever it might be—trivial, sublime, abject—and respects it for itself. This is what makes the image an instrument of choice for analyzing these "things," these objects we see, as well as their contemporary proliferation, as I shall show later.

In contrast therefore to a Manichean vision of the world, whether religious, moral, or radical, which in its different formulations is engaged in stigmatizing the "abuses by paintings and the indecency of images," the phenomenological sensibility or the imaginal perspective allows us, on the one hand, to be attentive to objects or events in themselves, in all of their own concreteness, presence, and dynamism. On the other hand, rediscovering an ancient tradition, close both to the Pre-Socratics and to the Far East, this perspective refuses *separation* in all realms—words and things, nature and culture, body and spirit—and is engaged in considering them in their globality, in their entirety. By this very fact it is among the most pertinent vectors of knowledge at a time when one is confronted by a galloping heterogeneity, and at the same time by a solid unicity ("it holds good," "it works"), both of which are characteristic of complex or organic societies. It is in this sense that distrust of images, which was an important trump card in the development of the rationality of modernity, is now totally inadequate for grasping the hyperrationality of postmodernity.

In addition, it is interesting to note that all the epochs in which an important caesura took place saw an upsurge, if not of the same problem, at least of an equivalent question. Fear of the image, like a sea serpent, resurfaces regularly when one way of being-togetherness gradually cedes to another one, with the restlessness that this does not fail to generate. There is a moment of panic about this new and hence mysterious thing that is not well mastered and that will only gradually find its equilibrium: the image in its preservation, its decline, or its beginnings.

To illustrate this phenomenon, I have already cited the quarrel of the images in Byzantium at the beginning of the Christian era, and the Reformation at the moment when modernity was inaugurated. In the latter period, one could equally well refer to the conquest of the New World, and more precisely of Mexico by the Spaniards. This country had a strong civilization, and hence an ensemble of images that served as its reference points. For the conquest to be effective, real, and total, the clerics, both religious and secular, alongside and in concert with soldiers and politicians, were engaged in making triumphant the true image, against that which was only a "cursed effigy" whose seal was "imprinted on the skin and in the heart." Certainly such a struggle was not linear, and historians have shown the oppositions, nuances, and differences in valuation on the subject among the religious orders. However that may be, a certainty took hold little by little, as Serge Gruzinski strongly puts it, of "locating an image and recognizing the devil in it." Confronted with strange objects and representations, soon conscious of their import, the colonizers were well aware that their victory would not be total or even simply real until their own images replaced those that were worshiped locally. Hence the merciless struggle they undertook, that would only culminate with the annihilation of indigenous images or at the very least with their "baptism," specifically their recuperation, into the whole Christian symbolic system.[9]

This historical example illustrates the warlike version of the philosophical moralist or the theological distrust of the image, of images always "cursed and perverse" and their profusion. And, finally, the contemporary fear about appearances or the invasion of television and advertising is of the same stripe: as soon as some rational purpose exists, whether a paradise to be attained, a perfect society to be constructed, or a country to be conquered, one cannot accommodate oneself to what tends to anchor one here, or make the here and now appreciated and make passing time enjoyable, as well the objects that are vectors of such accommodation. The crystallizing image of all the aforementioned, the image totally indifferent to good and evil, the image well encapsulating this hedonism—should therefore be combated, or failing that, be replaced by another that can be better mastered or manipulated.

Thus, in summary, we are confronted by a major paradox: what allows the being-in-the world of each individual, or of any whole social ensemble, what grounds the being-togetherness of any political or social organization—in short, the image, the sight, the being seen—everything is suspect and potentially fiendish. To make use of certain popular sayings, it is a matter of the Devil's prerogative, master and possessor of that world, in opposition to the better celestial world; or in a more sophisticated manner, it is the property of the "earthly" Dionysus, a rooted divinity, in opposition to the son of light, the Uranian Apollo. In *Leonardo da Vinci and a Memory of His Childhood,* Freud remarks that this extraordinary creator of images is a painter "often giving the appearance of being indifferent to good and evil," and he gives various examples of this.[10] But at the same time, Freud recognizes that, precisely, one cannot measure the Creator by the standard of common mortals. In extrapolating the thesis, one might say that this amoralism is the very property of any image that does not seek

what ought to be, in general, but instead describes what is
lived here and now, and hence is not encumbered with models
to imitate or ideas to realize, follow, or apply.

It is perhaps just here that the heart of the problem lies: the
image is a form that seduces, that attracts, and that thus has
nothing to do with any moral injunction. Philosophical distrust, like theological iconoclasm or political stigmatization,
is in fact just a defense mechanism against the attraction of
what the Greeks called quite rightly the *phantasia* of visual
perceptions, since the property of these "fantasies" is precisely to be ungovernable, disordered, and somewhat savage.
Michel Foucault reminds us of the role placed by *phantasia* in
sexual pleasures: they serve not only to recollect them, but
also to perceive them. Thus he cites Plutarch who, with respect to the opportune moment for sexual acts, advised flee-
ing the light in order to avoid "images of pleasure" that "constantly renew our desire." Quite appositely, the question of
images in amorous literature underlines the fact that the look
is considered "the surest vehicle of passion." On this theme, I
refer the reader to Foucault's study in *The Care of the Self;*[11]
what is lived paroxysmally for the *aphrodisia,* these sexual
things whose management is quite difficult for any society,
also remains a problem for all the other aspects of social life.

This problem can be summarized in the following manner:
the *phantasia,* visual perceptions, the images upon which they
rest—all are really or potentially erotic, in the strongest sense
of the word (what unites me with the other, what fosters conjunction, copulation). Hence everything that arouses such
an attraction—whether the look, images, perceptions, recol-
lections—must be controlled and managed with prudence.
Every sexual economy, meaning the manner in which sex circulates, is summed up in this. In short, one could say that the
fear of the image rests essentially on its erotic charge, that it
takes one out of oneself and fosters attachment to the other.

Thus, at the very least within the Western tradition, we are attached to preserving the self, the ego, which on the model of the deity ought not to see itself, be seen, or favor appearances. "The essence of subjectivity is separated from the exteriority that distorts it." This formula of the philosopher Francis Jacques summarizes my proposition very adequately: everything that is exterior—and we are concerned here with an immense realm running from appearance to the body, including their images—is of the order of religious sin, philosophical distortion, moral imperfection. The ideal—according to the order of reality under consideration (theological, philosophical, moral)—is to reach the ascesis of the saint, the ataractic of the sage, or the apathy of the moralist.

Such a pressure does not remain without effects. Hence we can understand how the imaginal world remains, in part, unthinkable. It has too much to do with the sensory, with enjoyment in the present, with the relativism inherent in things here below. But at the same time, we see that what is so strange to those who function by the logic of ought-to-be is in perfect congruence with those who, attentive to popular wisdom, recognize precisely that nothing is absolute, but that everything is worth something only to the extent that it is in relation with the ensemble of people and things. It is this putting into relation in which the factual image, the ephemeral image, the sensual image is engaged. It is worth nothing in itself but, in a movement of reversibility, draws its force from every social in which it is integrated, from every social that it constitutes, that it evokes and epiphanizes with more or less beauty.

The Image as "Mesocosm"

In its relativism the image is thus an instant of globality, an instant of what we could call holism. This has long been a dynamic perspective of thought. If, as I have suggested, separa-

tion prevailed in Western tradition, it was not without a
struggle. In the Greek tradition, the division between *ratio*
and myth is much less comfortable than it initially appeared.
Thus, even with Plato and Aristotle, who could be counted
among the founding fathers of Western rationalism, we find a
close interpenetration between these two elements—myth
and rationality—that will later give rise to separate, even opposed, intellectual traditions. For example, with Plato the
myth of the *soul,* or with Aristotle the love borne by all things
for the "immobile motor of the universe"—each gives birth to
a most coherent philosophy. What is certain is that there is an
interaction between these two poles, an interaction that we
discover again among great thinkers, and which dogmatic
thought, often issuing from interpretations by epigones, is engaged in trying to separate. To take up Kant's formulation:
"Mythical thought without the formative *logos* is blind, and
logical theorizing without living mythical thought is empty."
Thus, when one looks at the history of thought over time, one
becomes aware that it is only gradually, and always imper-
fectly, that the rationalization of myth takes effect.[12]

But one could say that Plato the mystagogue, like all thinkers inspired by myth, being at the core of popular tradition, is
rooted in primordial globality. Perhaps it is this that we could
call popular wisdom: the union of sensibility and understanding. Certain people, such as J. G. Hamann, will see in the "images of popular language" the crystallization of such a union.
To play on a self-evident theological metaphor, there is a "transubstantiation of experience into image."[13] This expression of
Pierre Klossowski's rightly stresses the mysterious and sacramental aspect of imaged language, which thereby unites the initiated among themselves and makes visible an invisible
grace—which is to say, makes society. For my part, I will speak
of a sensible reason, a deeply rooted reason, a concrete reason
that, while being very close to the life of every day, is no less a

thinking about this life. The image in this sense is not an abdication of the mind; it is, on the contrary, an enrichment, a way of activating all the potentialities of the mind. This is useful to bear in mind when trying to appreciate the extraordinary explosion of the postmodern image. Rather than seeing it, as disgruntled minds continue to do, as the expression of a decadence of culture and thought, perhaps it would be more opportune to know how to recognize in it the return of a more complete, more concrete, spiritual life, one that lives all its potentialities and thereby makes a community.

The fact is that the image may favor both a "love of forms" (Elie Faure), a "love of matter" (René Huyghes), and a sensitive reason.[14] As the utopians have well demonstrated, it allows us, above and beyond mediations, to accede to a kind of direct knowledge, a knowledge issued from sharing, from the putting in common of ideas, of course, but also of experiences, modes of life, and ways of being. In this light, we could thus recall the link existing between the daily piety inspired by Franciscanism and the "iconophile swarming" on which it was based.[15] Perhaps this is the "Reign of the Spirit," or the "third state," that, in various ways, has haunted all utopian quests, thought, and practices. Regarding the studies by one of the most notable of them, Joachim of Floris, one could speak of "symbolic orgy." The phrase is pertinent: it shows the synergy that, thanks to the image, is established between passion and the mind's ways. Symbolic orgy allows the simultaneous valorization of the efficacy of images, the intuition of direct knowledge, and of the organization (for him, the elite of contemplative monks) that was going to embody the first two.[16] One is indeed in the presence of a global conception of the world that, beyond the different separations of distinguishing thought, stresses the organicity of the whole and the complementarity of the different elements of this whole. The image is a kind of "mesocosm," a middle world between the macro-

and the microcosm, between the universal and the concrete, between the species and the individual, between the general and the particular, whence comes its own efficacy and the stakes that it represents.

We see the use that could be made, if only allusively, of such a thesis. Symbolic orgy is more present than ever. Certainly the Reign of the Spirit is perhaps not the one promised by the different utopians who, up to and including Marx, succeeded Joachim. It is nevertheless possible to interpret in this light the profusion of images, the return of symbolism, the development of religiosity—all the phenomena that could be schematically grouped under the label of New Age, up to and including everything that smacks of the immaterial images favored by technological development; and hence one could see in all of this the realization of a third state of the world, no longer simply attached to the imperatives of warmongers or business executives, but announcing a reality that is otherwise spiritual, a form of union among men and women, less utilitarian but more mystical—in short, a reenchanted world in which, without worrying about politicoeconomic imperatives, or rather with the latter being realized in their proper spheres, true life is unfolding elsewhere: closer to social actors, in the secrecy of microgroups, in the sociability of neighborhoods, in the affective ambience of friendships, in the viscosity of religious, sexual, and cultural adherence—all things that have need of images serving as their catalysts. Therefore it is no longer a question of Utopias in capital letters, or of great rational systems, but of the small interstitial utopias specific to emotional epochs.

Perhaps here it is a matter of waking dreams—let us remember Walter Benjamin, who saw in them the omen of what was going to happen in succeeding epochs. However that may be, and whatever the assessment one makes of all the symptoms that I have just listed, whether as interstitial utopias or as realized decadence, it is necessary to have at one's disposal an instrument of analysis that is in congruence with them. It accomplishes nothing to stigmatize a priori, even less to deny a reality that, in any case, will find a form of expression all the stronger, or all the more perverse, for having been all the more repressed. It is better to go along with what is in the course of being born, "to know" (*connaître*, from *cum-nascere*) it, to give it theoretical status— in short, to face the gnostic challenge that each epoch throws at its scholars.

The answer is certainly in a "figurative sociology" (Patrick Tacussel) that, rooted in the tradition I have just sketched, would be in a position to think through the organicity and the globality in question, that is to say, a kind of thought that knows how to ally the rigor of the scientific (or at least academic) approach with the sensibility drawn from the very sources of life. When Goethe's Faust underlined that "grau ist alle Theorie," the grayness of theory, he merely recognized the separation and the abstraction that had detached knowledge from "the golden green tree of life." On the contrary, taking seriously the play of images and the defense of illustration— this is what could renew ancient memory's dream of globality.

Let us think in this respect of Scipio's dream, *Somnium Scipionis*, a lovely apologia in which Cicero tries to unite the *bios theoretikos*, the intellectual search of Greece, and the pragmatic spirit of the Romans; an attempt, as Franco Ferrarotti reminds us, "to unite the logic of understanding and that of action."[17] Whatever the terms one is going to ascribe to each of these poles, it is certain that their synergy remains a fine utopia of knowledge, especially when, just as was the case in the already mentioned traditions, it is possible that in various manners—myth analysis (Gilbert Durand), formism

(Michel Maffesoli), figurative sociology (Patrick Tacussel)—
one may realize it anew. This means to say that above and beyond abstract categories or the study of perfect substances or
essences, one could and one might know how to take reality
into account, in all its spontaneity, at the very least as a support to thought. This is what Canetti called, quite rightly, "the
reflected-upon image," or the symbol (in the strictest sense of
the term), that is the union of two elements, to wit, the union
of thought and of "the thing itself."

It is quite evident that this realized utopia would not be
systematic. The property of the "reflected-upon image" is
precisely that of making us aware of the plurality of the real.
One could show coherences, establish correlations, but it is
not possible to make systems with images. Perhaps this is just
what marginalizes all schools of thought that rely on them.
On the other hand, this union of thought and of "the thing itself" is completely pertinent for describing a complex world
where heterogeneity rules. The possibility of illustrating, of
naming, of describing, while it does not have the generalizing
virtue of the concept, still brings out the internal reason *(ratio
seminalis)* that animates each thing. To come back again to
Canetti, in *Crowds and Power,* that prophetic book about
our times, his analyses all rest on forms, images, things that
listen to things, in their particularity, while giving them the
breadth of "types" that might have a general value.[18]

Although this detour to the image as a vector of knowledge
may appear a little speculative, I thought it necessary to make
it, so triumphant is the stigmatizing attitude we know of. In
effect, "the living image" results, to use André Breton's definition, from a fortuitous bringing together of two poles as
distant from each other as possible. One immediately thinks
of dream and reality. Undoubtedly these two, in particular
during modernity, have been constantly separated. At the

most the poet was allowed to try to make a junction between them, as long as this did not lead anywhere. But it was evident that the dream, whether individual or social, was to remain a realm apart: in private life, in institutional religion, in the secrecy of nocturnal alcoves.

And now dreams are erupting into the public place: perhaps this is one of the marks of postmodernity. "The living image" becomes an incontrovertible reality that one can continue to deny but that one will not be able to keep at bay much longer. It takes on the force of law in what remains of the political; it resurfaces in the affirmations of ethnicity; it topples walls, the solidity of nation-states, and the arrogance of empires built on dogmas, thus revealing their fragility. In short, this "living image," this union of dream and reality, without being recognized for what it is, is everywhere on the agenda, and in this sense it allows us to understand the transfiguration of the old order that is taking effect in front of us. This might seem astonishing, so true it is that we continue to analyze this transfiguration in the classic terms of politicoeconomic analysis that gives a feeling of security to those who still want to be convinced of it. But this astonishment *(étonnement)* soon risks becoming, as the etymology of the word indicates, what follows thunder. In effect, while the social encephalogram appears quite flat, while utopias appear dead and millenarian promises no longer attract us, a quiet expectation is perceptible to alert minds. Perhaps it is a question of the calm that precedes the most violent storms, and whose noisy silence is made up of a multiplicity of small things that cannot be analyzed with the sole tool of reason. Here is where the image, isolated or in composition with others, the traditional image and the technologized one, are just like many indices that, without giving us a guaranteed direction, nevertheless indicate a general tendency.

The Linking Image

These days, the essential function that one could grant the image is that which leads to the sacred. It is, in fact, striking to see that outside all doctrines, and without organization, there exists a "faith without dogma," or rather a series of "faiths without dogma," best expressing the reenchantment of the world that, in various ways, strikes all social observers. For my part, I have spoken of religiosity contaminating, step by step, all of social life. In effect, it is no longer the religious domain, *stricto sensu*, that is at issue, but rather all religions "by analogy," which could mean sports, musical concerts, patriotic gatherings, or even opportunities for consumption. Now in each of these cases, and one could multiply the list endlessly, the "link" is established around images we share with others. It could be a matter of a real image, or of an immaterial image, or even of an idea around which one communes—it does not matter. On the contrary, what interests me here is that this "*cosa mentale*" has an efficacy that one cannot deny anymore.

Commenting on Durkheim, Serge Moscovici even speaks of a "resurrection of *imago*" that is acting profoundly on the body social. It might be a conventional emblem or symbol, a sign that is in principle banal, a trivial object or an anodyne word that, suddenly or on the occasion of a particular rite, becomes a totem, an "image of a sacred thing" (Durkheim). But in a movement of reversibility, these images both take on life and regenerate the body social—society or small tribal ensemble—that serves as their support. The flag, the "brightly colored rag," is going to give rise at that moment to an intense collective sentiment. A very ordinary word is going to achieve the "function of a sign" and become a means of recognition or serve as a rallying cry. In each of these cases, an image reinforces the social tie that thereby finds once again its "original vigor."[19]

The reference to Durkheim is not idle, since his notion of "collective consciousness"—provided one does not make it an intangible concept and a universal key—is quite pertinent for understanding contemporary society and its various effervescences, which all are effected around, or on the basis of, sentiments, emotions, images, symbols—causes and effects of this "collective consciousness." On this subject, Durkheim's position is very clear. Thus, for him—curiously for such a positivist—society is not constituted solely by this material thing that is the ground occupied by individuals, nor by the "things they make use of," nor "by the movements they make, but, above all, by the idea that [society] has of itself." In the same way, to make the importance and implications of this idea more precise, he again specifies that "collective consciousness is something else than a simple epiphenomenon with a morphological basis, just as individual consciousness is something else than a simple efflorescence of the nervous system." It is the result of a "synthesis sui generis" giving rise to sentiments, ideas, and images that "once born, obey the laws proper to them."[20]

Hence, while seeing religion as an essentially social thing, Durkheim does not hesitate to underline the specificity and the autonomy of the collective idea, which should be understood here as an immaterial aura that, issuing from society, will return toward it in order to constitute and comfort social life. One finds here the logical notions of "cause and effect" or "action-reaction" as used by contemporary sciences but working, if not to invalidate, then at least to nuance or relativize the causal mechanism that has prevailed throughout modernity. It should be understood that for Durkheim the religion he is describing is, above all, that impulse that links me to the other, which, following Marcel Bolle de Bal, one might call "linkage," that is to say, that mysterious cement—nonlogical, nonrational—that is not the effect solely of these exceptional moments—festivals, liturgies, rituals—with which religion is generally credited, but that is inscribed quite precisely in what the quotidian possesses of the most anodyne. It is what he calls "the irresistible authority of habit." Bolle de Bal even goes further along the line toward banality, by specifying that a "society without prejudices would resemble an organism without reflexes: it would be a monster incapable of living."[21]

Prejudice, opinion, good sense—we could find numerous expressions to designate that which scholarly thought has qualified, intending to invalidate it, as *doxa,* that unnameable thing that healthy and pure reason ought to have superseded. So it is interesting to see Durkheim refer to necessary prejudice, all the more since the latter (and this is what concerns us here) is most often expressed in images, sets of banal images that at the same time favor an undeniable communion. Personally, inspired by Gilbert Durand, I consider all the stereotypes that are at the basis of prejudices to be profoundly rooted in immemorial archetypes, always latent but taking on force at certain moments, becoming visible and playing, therefore, a central role in the strengthening of social ensembles of reduced size. Thus the rational idea is cause and effect of those great ensembles of modernity that are nation-states, and of which politics is the natural expression, whereas the imaginal idea might be the effect of those tribal or ethnic ensembles characteristic of postmodernity and which will find in the "domestic" their natural space.

As I have previously suggested, in the cyclical becoming of the world—perhaps it would be better to say the spiraling becoming of the world—this "archaic" thing that is the need for linkage, the impulse to be with the other—in short, social at-

traction—returns to the forefront with its retinue of aggregative images. In this sense, one could speak of the rebirth of a
Homo religiosus who would be just a variant of the *Homo
aestheticus,* that is, of the renaissance of a social individual
and a society resting not on distinction from the other, nor
any longer on a rational contract linking to the other, but
rather on an empathy that makes me, with the other, a partic-
ipant in a larger ensemble, contaminated all the way through
by collective ideas, shared emotions, and images of all kinds.
It is also what I propose calling the "imaginal" world.

This no longer has anything to do with the modern histori-
cism that envisaged human development either according to a
regular linearity or as the new foundation or renaissance of
what had been at the origin of a social ensemble. Similarly,
what can no longer be applied is the habitual critical attitude
that "overcame" individual and collective contradictions,
that made choices according to a hierarchy of well-estab-
lished values and thus acted as a function, not of the times
lived here and now, but in reference to the distant "what is to
come." Quite to the contrary—and on this point I am following the theoreticians of postmodernity—the imaginal world
rests on what Martin Heidegger called the *"Verwindung,"*
and what Vattimo proposed translating by means of terms
such as "reprise-acceptance-distortion," meaning the *reprise*
of archaic elements (archetypes, immemorial myths), the *acceptance* of what is (appearance, phenomenon, relativism),
and the *distortion* of these archaic elements—all entering into
a spiraling movement that makes them dynamic and gives
them a current meaning.

In this respect, it suffices to refer to postmodern culture,
whether architectural, pictorial, or cinematographic, to see
the three moments I have just mentioned at work.[22] The recol-
lection or *reprise* of the past, the *acceptance* of its compo-

nents, and the *distortion* they are made to undergo are particularly evident in postmodernist architecture that, in a manner
all the more caricatural when it is visualized in a clearly delineated building or district, best illustrates the three categories
just noted. In each of these cases, the long run or the faraway
with which one criticizes the present that is here gives way to
an acceptance, even if relative, of what is seen and of what is
lived hic et nunc—no longer history but the event.

The property of an event—which could be compared to
what Greek philosophy called the *kairos,* the sense of opportunity—besides its punctuating and ephemeral aspect, is that
it is intimately linked to the phenomenon it actualizes, that it
makes visible. Different forms of rites are, in this respect, illuminating. In addition, the very property of the phenomenon is
precisely that it has need of being seen, it has been constructed
as an image, to make things visible. This lets us understand
the relation that I have established between *Homo religiosus*
and *Homo aestheticus:* the sharing of the image, the aesthetic
that this gives rise to, generates relations, engenders linkages,
and, in short, favors religion.

One should not understand the latter in its organizational
or doctrinal form. To take up Simmel's distinction, one could
say that life engenders "sentiments and modes of behavior
that one is obliged to call religious, even if they are in no way
experienced under the concept of religion." This could mean,
he explains, love, impressions of nature, different ideals, or
communitarian senses—everything that engenders a religiosity that religion follows, more than it precedes it.[23] All these
elements—and this is their specificity—both belong to the
quotidian and express themselves along the vector of the image. Now it happens that sentiments, fashion, nature, and
their emblems and representations occupy a significant place
these days; they are even, under quite diverse variations, at

the heart of social life, and thereby, in fact, constitute the domestic passion that is succeeding political reason.

The junction between the religious and the "aesthetic" (by way of a reminder: that which favors shared emotion) is particularly evident in the paroxysmal forms that are the various ecstasies—in particular, musical, sporting, or touristic—that punctuate social life. All these occasions foster a getting out of oneself, a "bursting" into the other and by the other. Here again, the image is the vector of choice. In fact, most of the time, it is the image that fosters and comforts the trance. A trance, *stricto sensu,* means that of cults of possession, but it also refers to those minor trances, unrecognized as such, like military parades, excitation in nightclubs, dancing at dancehalls, large concerts of various kinds, or even the collective emotions experienced over fashion, sports, listening to a beautiful speech, or at all those gatherings, those many crowd events (*affoulements*) so common in postmodern megalopolises.

There is a "trance of the imaginary" of which the baroque gave us the capital example and that today is reborn with the "baroquization" of the world. The property of this trance, as I have said, is that it fosters the bursting of the self. Through the image I participate in this small other, which may be an object, a guru, a star, a painting, a piece of music, ambience, and so forth, and thereby a great Other is even created: society. Magic participation, which one had thought reserved to the primitives, comes back in a great rush with the reenchantment of the world. In this sense, the imaginal world, by the endless game of reversibility, favors a "correspondence" in the Baudelairean sense, a correspondence in which it is not just inanimate objects or different elements of nature that enter into composition with each other, but in which each and every one, by the joint participation in the cult of images, enters into resonance with others until a particular rhythm is created—so disturbing for social observers—that suddenly makes inner-city neighborhoods revolt or else some stratum, corporation, or socioprofessional category break off from the rest.

In each case, there is affective contagion: I feel myself other, and with the other I participate in a joint emotion that may be explosive or gentle, brief or dragged out at length, but that in every instance is intense, translating a very strong tribal organicity and best expressing the pregnant import of an image, or of an ensemble of images, in a given social body. Here we find what Lou Andreas-Salomé called a "retroactive effect," what in more modern language we would call the process of reversibility. We are miles away from the univocal approach of a history sure of itself, like the one rationalism has gradually imposed. "The real religious phenomenon manifests itself above all in the retroactive effect of a god—it matters little how it is born—on a person who believes in this god."[24]

It is quite evident that this "god" can be multiple. One could even say that one is confronted with a plurality of small gods, each more profane than the others, of which each is an emblem favoring aggregation. This is certainly the explanation of what it is convenient to call the bursting of the social, or its heterogenization: there is no longer a unique value and a truth that accounted for it by means of rational analysis but, quite the contrary, there is a multiplicity of values (fashions, ways of being, lifestyles) expressing themselves in a cacophony of ideologies, each more fragmentary than the others. And yet, this polytheism is not incoherent. All these disparate elements hang together, hence the metaphor of the *baroquization* of the world I have offered, since despite (or perhaps thanks to) this heterogenization, the different elements of the given social still constitute a solid organicity. The efflorescence of images is at once cause and effect of this organicity: they are diverse and multiple, but, entering into correspondence or into resonance one with another, they create a unicity, a cohesion that envelops life and the representations of each and every one.

Several times I have insisted on the idea of *kairos*, of opportunity, of a time that is not finalized but is lived in the present. An eternal present—toward this the image invites us. But so that there should be no misunderstanding, presentism, while it relativizes historical linearity, by no means signifies the negation of temporality. It quite simply stresses an atemporal time, it is an *illud tempus*—the time that is of today as well as of yesterday. In short, the time of myth, which, as Gilbert Durand has often shown, is not conceptualized but is a "bearer of images"—or rather, he does not demonstrate it, with the evolutionary process that demonstration never fails to possess, but is content with showing it (hence the repetitions, the redundancies that are inherent in "mostration").[25] There is always a conjunction of the aesthetic and the religious: myth, in showing, favors being-togetherness, the joint sentiment. The image that serves as its support links people to each other and links us to time immemorial, meanwhile accentuating the lived in its actuality and even its mundaneness.

In fact, the accent placed on myth, on the present, reminds us that the image that serves them as support is an essential element in any social structuration. Thus, before a society reorganizes its material life, before it elaborates an ideology of utility—in short, before it gives itself a politicoeconomic project or constitutes its power—that society has need of an immaterial strength, of the symbolic, the useless—things we could gather under the term *social imaginary*. In this respect, you only have to see the solidity and the strength of nascent societies, or else the dynamic aspect of the gatherings of youth or other groups (political, cultural, religious) that rely on a shared ideal. In each case, the living force of the given en-

semble is indeed the utopia, the imaginary that has constituted it. And it is when this imaginary is etiolated that the social structuration in question loses its force and tends to break
down.

By way of example, I would cite the prophetic speech given
by Walter Benjamin in 1914: he shows that students become
sterile, that the university no longer participates in the essential debates of the nation, when they forget their imaginary, to
wit, the utopia of disinterested knowledge, the search for culture for its own sake. It is what he calls the "denaturation of
the creative spirit into an occupational spirit." In effect, a student life "entirely subject to the idea of function and occupation," far from leading to a deepening of life, far even from
constituting a true apprenticeship to this life, is the very thing
that, by a direct and immediate utility, tends to lead to spe-
cialization, to reduce the view of the ensemble, and finally to
make the student just an interchangeable cog in the social machinery.[26] His analysis is pertinent, and even topical, and it
underlines especially well the necessity of aesthetic sentiment,
of sentiment for the useless, of the necessity for utopia, and
the strength of images in the constitution of a community
called upon to think and to act on society.

To be more precise, it is adequacy to the internal rationality,
to the *semen rationalis* (the *logos spermaticos* in Greek) that
turns the buried seed into a promise of beautiful fruits. Or in
other words, it is when an individual or an institution corre-
sponds, profoundly, to its own image that it is the most im-
pressive, that it is in a position to be the most effective. This is
what Oriental wisdom teaches us, as well as that well-known
apologia of Japanese archers who more surely reach their
target when they are concentrated within themselves. But one
also finds the same perspective within medieval thought. Thus
for Robert Grosseteste, a university chancellor who organized

the young Oxford colleges, from the "central core" radiates the force that creates the universe. In fact, it is God, of course, but starting from there he shows that it is from the interior that beauty is born, that it springs from a given body and does not come from outside. Beauty, here, is what gives life: it is like a "splendidness of forms." Thus, just as God is the perfect "form" from which everything ensues, a form that shines on and gives life, so the property of a formation, scholarly or religious, is to elaborate a beautiful form, individual or social, which *de sui,* from itself, will diffuse outward.[27] We find it in Saint Augustine's adage: "Boni de sui diffusi."

I could offer many examples along these lines, but it suffices to recall that the image is not merely a supplement of the soul, to be dismissed at will, something superficial at best, and at worst primitive or anachronistic, but that, on the contrary, it is at the very core of creation, it is truly a "forming form"— of the individual certainly, the image of self, but also of the whole social ensemble that is structured thanks to and by means of the images it gives itself and that it must regularly recollect. Even if it is not formulated in this way, both the self and the ensemble are going to live as founding archetypes; and their vitality will be measured by their fidelity to these archetypes. And when the latter lose their force, the body social or the individual body tends to be weakened, sometimes even to disappear, until other images come to regenerate the body in question.

One clearly sees, then, why I stress the linking of the image. In playing on the euphony of the word in French *(reliance)* and its English meaning, one could say that the image "links" *(relie)*; it bestows ties and secures all the elements of the worldly given. At the same time, it allows a certain *confidence* one must have in order to exist in what surrounds us, whether the social environment or the natural environment. By means of these various procedures, or the categories I have indicated, it might be said that the imaginary, images, and the symbolic give rise to the minimal confidence that permits the recognition of the self on the basis of recognition of the other, whatever the status of that "other" (individual, space, object, idea).

So it is the fact of being linked and the fact of having confidence that constitute, in its simplest meaning, the environment—what I like to call (to accentuate the fact that we are dealing with something that preexists the individual or the group) the social "given" or the worldly "given." One finds the same thing in Bruno Schütz, who uses the strong expression "taken for granted." Obsessed by doing, action, history and by their development, we have perhaps not paid attention to that world, to that environment. Or rather it has been taken into account, but merely as something static, an object one had to exploit, to manage, to master *(ob-jectum, Gegenstand)*. In recalling the imaginal charge of this "given" world, one gives it back its dynamic force. The environment rests on a correspondence, a reversibility: it constitutes a living milieu, it is "media-environment" (A. Berque) or "anthropological trajectory" (G. Durand).

Thus understood, the environment is not a merely inert thing. It is admittedly constituted by spatiality: there are places, monuments, streets, but at the same time, according to the hallowed expression, these places have a genius, the genius loci. This genius is given to them by one or several imaginary constructions, whether tales and legends, written or oral memories, novelistic or poetic descriptions. All this means that the spatial static is animated and animates: *stricto sensu,* we give it life and it vivifies. It suffices, in this respect, to notice the importance attached to notions like that of "country"or "territory," with the symbolic charge that is attributed to them, in order to measure the extent of this "animation."

With regard to the Holy Land, Halbwachs has shown the role played by imaginary topography. Nostalgia, the ideal or utopic have an efficacy that rational geopolitics would do well to recognize. Human history demonstrates its effect, and smoldering current events in the four corners of the world signal that a creeping phantom—which one had thought eliminated by means of treaties or boundary settlements (rational and centralizing)—such as the union of a "country" (static) and a symbolic (dynamic) is in fact a detonator of incalculable consequences. Here again we find an effect of that old mole, burrowing its subterranean galleries, that is the image.

Reference to space lived symbolically, to what I have called the "animation" of the country or territory, allows us to perceive the collective representations that make up the milieu in which one lives with others. This could mean the mythic representation of the ancient world or the scientific representation that prevails these days—the difference is not important. As Marcel Mauss reminds us, in the lineage of Durkheim's *Elementary Forms of Religious Life,* it is necessary to attribute a "preponderant role to the psychic element in social life, to collective beliefs and sentiments." Whether they are thought to be irrational, considered as illusions, whether they are the remnants of archaic beliefs, whether they are emotions or passions lived in realms as diverse as politics, sports, or the university, these collective representations play an un-deniable "symbolic" role; that is to say, they restore a form of globality where formerly there prevailed the separation and distinction between words and things, between social facts and individual facts, and among individuals themselves.[28]

Thus, the collective image that invests a place and makes space dynamic has the function of a matrix: it preserves, protects, and brings to the world. One is *of* a place as of one's childhood; it is from here that one may grow and prosper. But this place (just like the time of childhood) plays the role just mentioned if it has this "extra" accorded it by the social imaginary. The Chicago school was not mistaken about this, as one of its protagonists, Robert Park, knew when he declared that "communities are not, however, mere population aggregates . . . The city is not a formal and administrative entity . . . Ultimately the society in which we live invariably turns out to be a moral order in which the individual's position, as well as his conception of himself . . . is determined by the attitudes of other individuals and by the standards which the group upholds."[29] The city, he concluded, is a "state of mind." This is a judicious phrase that shows clearly that the materiality of a place is traversed by an ensemble of collective images giving it meaning. In a movement of action-reaction, space and image nourish each other—less for themselves, moreover, than in order to arouse, via the dynamic they thus create, the being-togetherness that is any life in society.

It is in this light that, in the strongest sense in which it is understood, the image *is* culture, the image *makes* culture: it is going to name the divinity of the peasant hearth as well as the town's patron saint; it is going to constitute the urban memory just like the roots of the rural home, in a word. Once again it is linking that is at issue; the image determines human behavior as a function of a given milieu, and at the same time, it fashions that milieu as a function of these human behaviors.

It is precisely this that I wish to bring out clearly. The lived and imagined space favors the thematic of "feeling with" so well developed by the romantics of the past century: to feel with the other, with others, or to "feel with nature" in its different variations. I have recalled that, above and beyond criticism, the image can refer back to what Heidegger called the *Verwindung*: the reprise, acceptance, and distortion of ar-

chaic elements in a contemporary situation, and an actualization in the present. After the example of space, one might add
that, in the lineage of romanticism, the image, above and beyond the critique of the sacred, favors what Friedrich
Schleiermacher called an "aesthetic of religion"—an expression which is redundant, since *aisthesis* and linking rest essentially on common sentiment, the "feeling with."

We could say that this "feeling with" is what constitutes the
ambient religiosity characteristic of postmodernity. In effect,
the religious link is no longer at all confined to institutions or
places formerly reserved for it. In paroxysmal cases, for example in Islam, it will occupy the whole of life and even make
the distinction between private life and public life disappear.
In another manner, it can become capillarized in the body social in the form of sectarian development. It is equally well
found, in latent form, in those "tribes" that (in all domains—
political, university, cultural, or simply amicable) riddle the
social tissue. In this case, the guru, the doctrinal chief, the political leader, or the influential intellectual is going to be set up
like any image around which people assemble, that is venerated and that one tries to protect and to disseminate.

This religiosity of "feeling with" and the determining role
the image will play in this are expressed also in the private
"cults" of different ludic rituals (lotteries and many games of
chance), in astrology, charms and amulets, clairvoyance, or
other cultures of nature, from ecology to macrobiotics, via all
forms of the New Age—that all favor fusion around the celebration of the cosmos in its globality. Here again, the rationalism of modernity has little hold, whereas the imaginary,
often accompanied by technological rationality, is the determining element of the social structuration.

Finally, you will find the aestheticoreligious "feeling with"
in the perseverance of symbols and small cult spots at the

very heart of great megalopolises, or in places (airports, factories, department stores) that seem a priori little propitious to the effusions they arouse. Without speaking of countries such as Brazil where syncretism and an exacerbated religiosity foster a multitude and especially a dramatization of such phenomena, it has been shown that even a country such as Japan is full of cult spots. For example, a war god of the tenth century, Taira no Masakado, is venerated in a small temple in the Otemashi business district of Tokyo; the god of commerce, Inani, has his altar at the tops of department stores; and the major industrial group, Mitsubishi, has a sanctuary in Osaka, its place of origin—many are the examples along these lines.[30] The "business shrines" (Kigyo, Jinja) are in this respect very interesting, since they testify to the survival I am speaking of. But still more, they show how an economic domain that Western Taylorism had totally removed from the order of collective emotions and sentiments is in fact totally riddled with them—which the enterprise culture would seem timidly to acknowledge more and more. One might even conclude that the competitiveness of Japanese firms rests precisely on the fact that (magic) participation in the house image and the religiosity this induces both lead to a devotion, sometimes even to a total subordination, to the factory, office, or university of which one is a member and to which ones makes a gift of one's person.

One could endlessly pursue the list of these situations, phenomena, and ambiences that take good account of the pregnant import of the image (aesthetic) and of its force of attraction (linking). For the moment, we may simply consider them as so many paths of a search that ought to incite us to think of the transfiguration of postmodern societies: descended from the heaven of ideas, images have contaminated, for better or worse, the whole of daily life.

"The Imaged Object"

The transfiguration of postmodern society finds its ultimate realization in daily life. In fact, the latter used to be, at worst, an object of reification (Georg Lukács), at best an object subject to criticism (Henri Lefebvre), and in any case the locus of a materialism that one could enjoy with some shame, but that one ought, at least in theory, to sublimate. It was not always thus, and we can imagine that it will not always be the case. It seems to me in effect that the image, of which we have noted the major characteristics, is engaged in spiritualizing matter, or rather in bringing forth from this matter the spirit of which it is full.

I have spoken of the baroquization of the postmodern world, and we recall that there exists a baroque conception of matter, which is totally different from the mechanistic way of analyzing it in modernity, thus relativizing the moralistic stigmatization that is in general applied to matter. Here I mention Gilles Deleuze, who well defines this baroque conception as testifying to a "generalized organicism, or to a ubiquitous presence of organisms (Caravaggio's painting?). Secondary matter is clothed, with 'clothed' signifying two things: that matter is a bouyant surface, a structure endowed with an organic fabric, or that it is the very fabric or clothing, the texture enveloping the abstract structure."[31]

In the second case, matter *is* organic; it is a structure composed of a multiplicity of elements that it combines with each other. All the elements, even the most anodyne and the most microscopic, enter into interaction with each other and compose by this very interaction the texture in question. To return to an expression I often use regarding what I call "formism": form is forming, or else form becomes vital force. One sees clearly how this baroque conception of matter can help us to

understand the contemporary *social tissue:* it is not solely
elaborated on the basis of a distant purpose, or an ideal to be
attained, a program to be realized, but quite to the contrary, it
is constituted on the basis of a close material life, made up of
anodyne and concrete things, in which meanings, sentiments,
and emotions have a role to play. To be more precise, we
could say that just as in the baroque, matter, as a force, was illustrated in the form of paintings, statues, or churches, nowadays it is the image as a covering sufficient unto itself that is
the metaphor of matter.

There could be many ways of analyzing this "matter" these
days—for example, when it is illustrated in cultural works
(painting, architecture, sculpture)—but, faithful to my
method of remaining attentive to the anodyne, to what is not
(or little) analyzed, I would like to show that it is *the object*
that may be, nowadays, a modulation of matter. There is the
noble object, the one in which we invest affectively the memory of happy moments or intense relationships; there is also
the useful object, without which social life no longer has
meaning, but also, in order to render the analysis more pertinent, the superfluous object, the gadget, the worthless bric-a-
brac that tends to abound in the temples of consumption, or
in the discount stores that are proliferating in our megalopolises. Coming back to "the thing itself," taking it seriously, and not seeking a remote meaning that it could, or
ought to, have: if I apply this perspective here, and do not suspect the object a priori or turn it into the contemporary form
of sin, then perhaps one will see in it a crystallization of
dreams, of images—in short, of the desire for the infinite that
always gnaws at the human being.

It may seem astonishing to connect object and image or to
see in the proliferation of objects one of the manifestations of
the strength of the image. I would like to point out that it is

not the only such manifestation, but it is not negligible. Closest to its etymology, the notion of "object" designates what is there, placed or thrown in front of me, hence a visible place that can be noticed, that I can imagine and see. By extrapolating or enlarging this thesis, one can say that this is what struck Arthur Schopenhauer when he said "thus the world is representation," noting that this position was the result of an "empirical realism associated with a transcendental idealism."[32] The philosophical terms used do not matter; it suffices to note, in this phrase, the synergy existing between the *thing* that one cannot help seeing and the *idea*, in its encompassing sense (transcendentalism), that takes account of it.

In addition, my hypothesis is that the object, as an element of matter, is a piece, or more precisely a modulation, of what Gilbert Simondon calls "preindividual reality," a reality that, just like objects, each of us contains. Hence the attraction, the correspondence, or even the (almost magical) participation in these objects is a way of reintegrating that "preindividual reality" that individuation, inherent in socialization, had divided up.[33] The object in this sense would be a reminder of the *materia prima* from which we are fashioned. Indeed there is in this memento a conjunction of realism, of what is empirically realized, and of idealism, of what it makes me think of, what it allows me to hope for, and thereby the participation it induces. Thus understood, the object is near to that other thing that is the archetype: an immemorial image that bores into every individual and collective spirit. In a relation of reversibility that is well known, the object could indeed be the stereotype that temporally exhausts the force that it has drawn from the atemporal archetype. From this, it would not be paradoxical to see in the object the constant anamnesis of a *collective reality* to which, in a nonconscious manner, we continue to aspire. Whether the latter is a primitive community, the warmth of the matrix, uncorrupted nature, earth without woe, or any other form of utopia does not matter at all; it seeks expression, coming to light, making itself seen. The object and the image would then be two sides of the same exigency.

Hence the object as a reminder of a primordial image. This is what would explain the fetishistic attachments that one bears toward it or all the projections to which it gives rise. Thus, without neglecting the different psychoanalytic interpretations, one could best understand the intimate relations that can be entertained just as much with furniture and family heirlooms as with one's automobile, pen, or libidinally invested clothes. The list is long of these "things" (see Georges Perec) that comfort an image of my ego by the communion that I establish with the images of the world. We can agree, however, *a minima*, on the fact that these "things" favor a projection outside of the individual monad and so turn each one of us into an element in the collective whole. This is what may allow us to explain why one does not possess such-and-such an object, but rather is possessed by it. This "alienation" is perhaps no longer to be explained, in moralistic terms, as the expression of a mercantile reification but, on the contrary, as a magical participation in a more vast ensemble: I become a stranger to myself, which makes me enter wholeheartedly into the community of others. In my opinion, a number of effervescent attitudes, a whole series of mimeticisms—in short, all the processes of *fashion* whose importance we increasingly recognize in all domains—find their root there: by means of objects I am alienating from myself and losing myself in others.

Thus the object, be it the most inert one, introduces us to the living world of communion. The cult of images in the Catholic Church played exactly this role: the statue, to which one owed only a cult of "*dulie*," integrated us into the vast "communion of saints," a communion with those who were living, but also a communion with those who had preceded us into the Kingdom of Heaven. One could say the same thing of the communion induced by the objects of mass consumption: they introduce us, collectively, into a terrestrial kingdom, much more ephemeral and tragic than the Christian paradise—but after all, each epoch has the paradise that it can have (or that it deserves). It suffices, for those of us who realize it, to recognize here a "spiritual trait of the inanimate" that, by a curious inversion, introduces into the world some social animation. Is it not this that "commerce" initially signified?

In effect, alongside the commerce of ideas (ideology), there is the commerce of goods (economy), and the commerce of the body (sexuality). Each of them governs objects, favors their exchange, their circulation, and thus contributes to the overall animation of social life. But this multiform commerce could not be put into relation, and this spirit that comes to objects and through objects—all this could take place only because it is "informed by" images. Organic matter is, in the strongest sense of the term, informed: the image puts into form, puts in order, puts into relation. We have seen the archetypal aspect of the relation object-image (stereotype-archetype), and we should be equally attentive to its contemporary expression: there is no product without an image that makes it be known and allows it to be disseminated and sold. Nothing escapes this putting into form: the industrial product, of course, but also the literary, religious, and cultural "product." It is the same with a town, region, or country that "is illustrated" in this way and that by an interposed "logo," slogan, or other design intends to give itself an image that leaves traces and favors its external dynamization and its internal animation.

Thus the object put into *form,* that is, the object that is spiritualized in an image, may be understood as a search for the
primordial, the archaic, the "preindividual reality" underpinning every society. We have difficulty understanding this,
since we are so much used to considering the image as a simple reproduction, or transfer, whether of the visible or of an
invisible idea (or ideal). Perhaps, to understand the import of
object-image, one should refer to a notion circulating among
the indigenous peoples of Mexico, the *ixiptla* that, according
to Serge Gruzinksi, stresses the immanence of forces proper to
the image. "The *ixiptla* is the receptacle of a power, the locat-
able and epiphanal presence," the actualization of a force in-
fused in an object, a being-there, "without any distinction between the divine essence and the material support" being
made in the minds of indigenous peoples.[34] For them, by
means of the object—some representation of the divinity, for
example—the divine force rises up, acts, becomes opera-
tional. In this sense, the collective body is made dynamic by
the very force of the celebrated image, by the force of some
object that is venerated. By analogy, I would say almost the
same thing about the contemporary object-image: in possess-
ing it, or in being possessed by it, one evades the self, the contingencies of the world, in order to attain a pure materiality,
to participate in the strength of basic material things of the
worldly given. The postmodern man who caresses his car,
who is fascinated by his videocassette recorder or other objects of that type, is similar to a primitive who by touching
some talisman, or by paying handsomely for the purchase of
some finery made of shells, participated in the primordial
strength of the surrounding world. By doing so, it is a sort of
communion that is installed.

It is a communion with nature, but also a communion with
others. At the risk of being tiresome, one must insist on this

communal dimension of the object, since in truth its reifying aspect has up until now been especially underlined or else the logic of imprisonment that the object induced. Certainly this reification and this imprisonment were the characteristics of modernity, procedures that had been well analyzed by what was called Western Marxism, by Lukács in particular, or else in a more forceful way by the Situationists (Guy Debord, Raoul Vaneigem) during the 1960s; it is also in the same lineage that we could classify Baudrillard's *system of objects*, which has widely disseminated this perspective. We could summarize it by citing Deleuze, who declares that "we isolate, purify or concentrate the object, we cut all its ties to the universe . . . we put it into contact . . . with an Idea"; he well defines the tactic of separation or cutting off characteristic of modern Western society. But sometimes, Deleuze continues, "on the contrary, the object is broadened according to a whole network of natural relations", the object "itself overflows its frame."[35]

Extrapolating this hypothesis, I would say that the separated and separating object gives way to a unifying object, and this continues along until perhaps it is the world in its entirety that becomes a pure object: the "objectal" world, meaning a world that has pushed the logic of the artificial so far that this logic has become its very nature. It is a world in which the object, and the image expressing it and serving as its support, on the model of the pure and brute materiality of nature, together design a new harmony, in which the animate and inanimate enter into synergy and end up in an equilibrium, sometimes conflictual, sometimes somewhat monstrous, in which everything is in its place and occupies it well. In this respect, it suffices to refer to the swarming of people and things that characterizes certain areas of our big cities in order to appreciate the pertinence of this hypothesis. I will not come back in detail to this description, but I have already shown how, by taking the example of a street in Tokyo, New York, or São Paulo, one could see a specific sociality being sketched on the basis of the "aura" that emerges from the accumulation of objects. One could show something similar through the "supermarkets" or shopping centers of various kinds that proliferate these days, and which, beyond the simple functionality of products, engender a specific ambience in which the role of the image is far from negligible.

Research under way on "commercial centers" or shopping malls, as much in Paris as in Rio de Janeiro or Montreal, well demonstrates the sociality that impels them. It also shows, beyond the simple utility of objects, the symbolic role that the profusion of objects does not fail to play, and especially the merchandising and advertising with which they are adorned. Here again, the object enters into an undeniable "animation," and one only need think of the Forum des Halles in Paris to understand in what way, really or fantastically (meaning by going there or by participating there via the interposition of reputation or television), the inert object, made dynamic by the image, gives impetus to an undeniable vitality whose effects still remain to be analyzed. Moreover, it is not insignificant that we baptize these centers with names reminiscent of antiquity: Agora, Forum, Polygons, and so on. It is the archaic "commerces" of which I spoke (goods, speech, sex) that are unfolding in them. The postmodernist architecture that is taking hold of them, such as that of Ricardo Bofill in Montpellier, may give the impression of a "pasted-on decor," and with cause, since a vast theatricality is being offered there, with its grandiose scenes (street spectacles) or banal ones (the daily routine), with its typecast actors in flamboyant costumes (the diverse urban tribes) or its habitual strollers. In the end, all this constitutes a series of fleeting, noisy, multicolored images, giving that "intensification of the life of nerves" that was, according to Simmel, the characteristic of modern metropolises but that tends to become exacerbated in the postmodern megalopolises.

So there is indeed an aesthetic of the quotidian that begins with objects and then is nourished by their merchandising. But here one should take "aesthetic" in the (etymological) sense that I have often recalled: that which makes me feel the sentiments, sensations, and emotions of others. Design, advertising, the media, nonstop Muzak, and fashion in its different acceptances all show the conjunction of the inanimate and the animate, all express the synergy, growing stronger and stronger, between the object and the image. The design of domestic objects, for a long time neglected, at least in France, is perhaps the simplest expression—in any case, the most evident—of this aesthetic of the quotidian. The well-known principle according to which "unattractiveness doesn't sell" inspired American designers in the postwar period, but now one could say that it is the ensemble of housewares and domestic objects that enter into such a process.[36] The very fact of speaking about "industrial art" is no longer exceptional. Thus, it is natural these days to think aesthetically about the object that one produces, that one sells, that one buys. And from the viewpoint that I intend to develop here, this aesthetic, this "skin of things," constitutes an important part of the "skin" of the body social. By making an epiphany of things, by adorning them, by making a spectacle of them, it is in some way the body social that one celebrates by means of these pieces of matter that thus become elements of culture— a culture that in the strong sense of the word permits, grounds, and comforts social being-togetherness.

Evidently we are concerned with a being-togetherness that does not owe much to the active attitude that has prevailed throughout modernity. This is why, when we use the term *so-cial "actor,"* we should understand it less as someone who *acts* than as someone who plays, in front of others, some role. I have already indicated that the possessed "object," or one that possesses its owner, could be compared to the material images of the primitives, which had the magic function we know about and which engendered those "possessions" so shocking to the eyes of civilized man. In each of these cases there is a "participation" in a transcendence: strength of nature, power of the machine—in short, the force of materiality, brute or domesticated. But what is important at the moment is that this "participation" leads to what I have called an immanent transcendence, that is to say, that which transcends individuals, "is made immanent" in the group, and is going, in the strongest sense of the word, to constitute a tribe, with the dependence of some upon others that this never fails to involve.

This is the "communal" aspect of imaged objects. And let us even dare use the word: it is a new style of Eucharist. One can easily verify this with communication by crowds: the great department stores on Sundays and holidays constitute the places of assembling and meeting, instead of the traditional places of worship (temples, churches). People get together there as families, to do the weekly shopping, then have lunch at one of the restaurants of the mall or commercial center, with the festive aspect that remains attached to a meal taken outside the home. You go there to run across friends, neighbors, acquaintances from work; it is a good way of creating new links or of tightening those that had become distended. Or even more simply, one goes there "to touch another," to brush up against strangers, to participate in that tactile connectedness that is so little studied because it is nonverbal, but which counts for a lot in contemporary crowd situations.

The Eucharist metaphor could be equally well applied to the diverse gatherings taking place around one of those "imaged objects" such as a rock singer, a sports team, a star intellectual, or even a religious preacher (the TV evangelists, for example), not to mention the Pope, of course, and the trips that take him in great pomp to the four corners of the world. In each of these cases, the inanimate imaged objects animates a community.

One could equally well apply this schema to the televisual image. I will content myself with sketching it here, indicating that just like the house of God, whether it be some particular church or the Church in its catholicity, the television screen favors a sort of community. This could be the community of those who in a precise place (house, café, public place) come to watch television together, but it could also be the invisible community of all those who, within one country or even throughout the world, go to vibrate in unison to the vicissitudes and reversals of fortune of the hero of a current serial. The image, in this case, assures a function of "copresence" all the more important in that it transcends frontiers and breaks through different barriers of nation, class, and ideology. The eucharistic aspect applied to television could again find many other illustrations: advertising, great charitable emotions (for the third world or the great humanitarian causes), various campaigns for ecological awareness, and so forth. All this gives rise to an "intense bombardment of images" that makes community, and this either for the best (mobilization for some elevated ideal) or for the worst (belligerent or racist masses, the stigmatization or eviction of minorities).

Whichever it may be, the magic strength of the image is essentially an aggregative force; it favors viscosity, and, as I will show later, fascination. It creates mystery, whose function (as a reminder) is to unite the initiated with each other, to foster recognition among those who feel themselves as such. One finds a note in this vein from Karl Marx (in a letter to Kugelmann on 27 July 1871) when he declares: "Up to now it has been thought that the Christian myth-building during the Roman Empire was possible only because printing had not yet been invented. Precisely the contrary. The daily press and the telegraph which spread their inventions over the whole earth in a second fabricate more myth . . . in one day than could formerly have been done in a century." What we could say of our own times when news and telegram are relayed by many other long-distance instruments, *telos* (television, telephone, telecopier)! These have relegated to the museum the old interdiction of images *(Bilderverbot)* and are on the way to multiplying myths infinitely. This is how we should understand this "intense bombardment of images."[37]

At the risk of shocking, I will say that this bombardment via the instruments of *telos* fosters the multiform reenchantment of the world that we observe today, with the upsurge of the communitarian (tribal, ethnic, identitarian) that is inherent to it. It is here that the aggregative force of the image, its viscosity, meets up with fascination. I have often indicated that nonactivity does not signify passivity. Or else that there is a way of expressing the sovereignty over existence, meaning a form of creation, that in no way comes under the province of modern "activism." The image could allow us to clarify this perspective. In effect, it simultaneously fosters a form of sensibility, of sensations, of shared sentiments, while at the same time it engenders a sort of impassivity. This may appear paradoxical, but there is in this *coïncidentia oppositorum* a summary of the whole contemporary dynamic: a global stability conjoined to a multitude of passionate micromovements regularly engendering strong social, ethnic, or corporate turbulences. The whole tragedy of politics is found here: deluded by the apparent calm that governs social life most of the time, politics is incapable of foreseeing the "rough seas," brief but periodic, that come along to punctuate the calm preceding storms.

This notion of *impassivity, apatheia,* is found among the mystics. It is a very paradoxical term since it signifies an "impassive passion, and designates a state that is maximally passionate, since it awakens the spirit from its drowsiness and turns one into an awakened person."[38] It is possible that this "impassive passion" may be at the very heart of postmodern social life. Regarding the object and the image, I have spoken of the dialectic between the inanimate and animation. Something of the same order is also happening in the paradox now under consideration. On the one hand, the bombardment of images and the various fascinations that this unfailingly produces together engender a sort of stupefaction, an acceptance of what is, a love of the nearby, of what is seen—in short, to take up a Nietzschean expression, an "affirmation" of life; one is engaged in "yeah-saying" acquiescence. This impassivity is expressed at best in the withering of politics. On the other hand, images and their fascinations engender an intense passionate participation via the multiplication of small passionate groups (tribes) in all domains or via the periodic explosions tearing holes in the tissue of a rational and well-regulated social, and setting aflutter various political, economic, or social leaders, who are powerless faced with a lack of "reasons" for these passionate effervescences. These passions, in turn, well display the transfiguration of the political.

What is certain is that the "imaged object," the sentiment of participation that it induces, the impassivity that is its consequence—everything must incite us to think that another temporality is being put in place, or rather is currently being reborn. I have already suggested that it is a time of myth, a time of nostalgia and of the already-lived. The sense of the present grounds itself in the event more than in the structures or institutions functioning over the long duration. A cinematographic expression puts this well: *freeze frame (arrêt sur image)*. This does not stop there being in this freeze frame, in the suspense it induces, a proper dynamic, an intrinsic force, that of passion, which does not fail to engender the well-known effervescences. Kierkegaard and Benjamin, each in his own way, spoke of a "dialectic of immobility." Here is yet another paradox that well translates that short circuit of opposing perspectives, or rather of perspectives that modernity had thought or willed as such: structure, intangible eternity, and history in perpetual movement. It happens that the end of the great narratives of reference and the saturation of the various certitudes that had guided social life attract our attention to reduced sequences of time. This is what the present is, the *object or the image as time that is contracting in space*. Hence the attention to the minuscule, the anodyne, the detail, the quotidian—and one could infinitely extend a list in this vein. For my part, I have summed this up by speaking of the transformation of the political into the domestic. It is precisely the focus on the domestic that permits overcoming the antinomy between eternity and history. As Adorno said of Benjamin's approach, "Through his concentration on the very smallest, . . . the historical movement halts and becomes sedimented in an image."[39]

The image is "Einsteinized" time, time that contracts. In this sense the love of the distant, of the city or life to come—in other words, the political—becomes the love of the nearby, of what is here, of what is seen (the image), of what is touched (the object, the other)—that is to say, the domestic. It is this inversion, this *transfiguration* that fosters various attachments—to territory, to objects, to nearby and local relations, to various "villages" or tribes of which we are members on more than one level—and so on in all domains. It is the very thing that engenders religiosity and the symbolism of which social life is filled, and that means that the latter no longer obeys the rationalist injunctions of politicoeconomic dominance. At the same time this engenders fervor, even if it is a limited fervor, or a fervor that is exclusive and thus excluding. In contrast to the "disenchantment of the world" (Max Weber), that mark of modernity, there is *pietas* in the mood of the times, "piety devoted to what has only a limited value," but by that very fact, beyond abstractions, beyond great intellectual and political machinery, a piety that is "love borne toward the living and its traces."[40]

A concept is general and universal. It wants to be effective and intends to serve some purpose. From this perspective, knowledge and power are one and the same. In contrast, the image, without caring about productivist effectiveness, is lazy and makes lazy, it favors that *otium* (the opposite of trade, *negotium*) that is a form of studious leisure, of wasting time, a succession of useless moments. Here one sees an important change whose outlines we have not finished studying but that certainly is going to determine another form of sociality.

Transfiguration by Images

To put it crudely, postmodern sociality is transfigured by images, on more than one count. If one sticks to the classic definition, transfiguration is the passage from one figure to another. In addition, it is in a certain (albeit minimal) manner close to possession. It is when one is "possessed," by a love, a divinity, or a feeling, that the body or the face is transfigured, that it takes on another dimension. One could ask whether, by virtue of the dialectic between quantity and quality, by accumulation, the world of objects is not transfigured into something else, or even whether the proliferation of images of all kinds does not end up creating a body social that escapes all the material, economic, or political contingencies that had constituted it up until then. One rediscovers here the notion of the "glorious body" of Christian tradition or that of the "body of light" dear to Iranian Sufism. They mean that a material entity operates a transmutation that makes it change into its contrary. In our case, individual bodies that are adorned, "dolled up," that are constructed, to which one applies an overabundance of cosmetics—and bodybuilding salons, hairdressers, and clothing styles all prove this—these bodies are therefore spiritualized, "angelicized." You only need look at the vogue for dieting, the quest for youth that is all the rage, the development of meditation, or various New Age techniques in order to be convinced of this. Whim or fantasy? It matters little, since for the social observer it is sufficient for something to exist for it to have its legitimacy. The myth of *Puer Aeternus* belongs to the list. Naive and impudent, pure and perverse, it has all the characteristics of the child who, because he is close to animal nature, plays with his body and can make a spectacle of it, but because he is inserted into civilization is going to make this body speak, make it conscious of itself, give it spirit.

Advertising, music videos, pop stars (our postmodern mythologies) are interesting in this respect, since they often dramatize ethereal and ambiguous androgynes, endowed with a body of eternal youth, and thereby they even serve as emblems for the craziest desires and for dreams that one can no longer describe as hidden, since they are proclaimed in the mimeticism of fashion, in the health cures and other manifestations of the ambient "youth cult." One remembers the evangelical advice: "Unless you become as children you will not enter the Kingdom of Heaven." After two centuries of accounting logic, in which the economy of the world dominated things like the economy of the self, it seems that in a few decades all these values are being inverted. At first it was the liberation *of* bodies and sexuality that then resulted in the liberty *enjoyed by* the body and sexuality, which is significantly different. The former is still within the instrumental logic that is going to make use of the body or of sex, while the latter tends to unburden the body and sex; it does not instrumentalize them, nor does it overcome them, as a certain moralism would have us believe, but makes them simpler, meaning that they are lived in themselves, for themselves, while accentuating the *present,* the event—in a word, the living. Thus experienced, this body and this sex express a sort of purity that is situated well beyond the anguish of sin, of a sense of guilt, and other logics of the ought-to-be that this never fails to arouse. Trivial expressions like "feeling good in one's body," "feeling good in one's head," or in a French slang phrase, "feeling good in one's tennis shoes" are illuminating in this respect. In effect, they take good account of the solidity and at the same time the casualness of a bodily posture that cannot be separated from an intellectual, even spiritual, attitude.

By a form of transubstantiation, we could say that the mental springs from the material. Thus in her *Reflections on the Problem of Love,* Lou Andreas-Salomé compares the process that I have just described to "the birth by which the vast universal matrix of physiology spawns psychic life."[41] This refers to a general idea that applies well to erotic drunkenness, but that one may, without fear, extrapolate to the hedonistic and Dionysiac ambience that in certain epochs encompasses everyday life. Ours is certainly one of these epochs, and thus it is that this transubstantiation becomes quite ordinary. In many respects this makes barriers porous and the separations between dream and reality, nature and culture, body and spirit more fragile. In effect, it is characteristic of this "psychic life," of this "mentality" that gushes from matter, from the body, and changes them into quite another thing, to be indeed encompassing and restore in an organic fashion the globality that rationalism had sliced up.

Such a transfiguration is perceptible in all domains: politics, business, daily life, consumption, tourism, services. There is no aspect of social life that is not contaminated by the image and that therefore does not install or restore the globality I have just mentioned. It could be the company ethos *(esprit maison)* or the enterprise culture; it could be the quest for the qualitative in current life or even the concern for the local in politics, not to mention advertising addressed to consumption. In all these cases, outstripping the brute materiality that constituted them, the image makes them undergo an enormous change that certain of them—I am thinking of politics in particular—risk not recovering from. In effect, by remaking the unity between "corpus" (the body, industrialized product, commercialized product, local community) and "spirit" (qualitativity, sense of beauty, disinterested caring, pleasure in the sensual, stress on the nearby and neighboring), the image realizes the stakes of the figurative tradition, which is to put the accent on the hedonistic, ironic, and aesthetic dimenion of existence. The problem is in fact extremely simple: from the moment that there is no beyond, or when goal and purpose are relativized, the only thing that matters is the present and its enjoyment. It seems to me that up to and including the enterprise culture, it is this quest for a "presentist" qualitativity that is at issue. One understands better, on this basis, how a politics that rests on the postponement of enjoyment, that is essentially oriented toward the future, will have difficulty in integrating the "imaginal" perspective; or rather, if the virus of the image can be integrated (through ads, enterprise culture, design) into production or consumption, it risks, on the other hand, destroying in its totality the body politic by derision, indifference, distancing irony—which seems the case nowadays.

In short, the image—from popular imagery, including comic strips, to immaterial images—has always been a place of refuge, a way of experiencing dissidence, the expression of that utopia, always renewed, that is the quest for a perfect society or, at the very least, for a society in which the weight of constraint and necessity would be less heavy. Whence come the dreams, desires, and fantasies that it never ceases to arouse, and which every kind of power—ecclesiastical, political, intellectual—has always mistrusted. The "beautiful escape" is inscribed at the very heart of the image; it always refers back to an elsewhere supposedly better, that one may live in a major key in moments of revolt, revolution, or important change, or an elsewhere that one may live in a minor key, or homeopathically, in the cinema, the comic strip, advertising, or the feeling of belonging to a "in-house" subculture.

In this sense, the image is by no means a duplication of reality, nor is it the reflection of an infrastructure to which all reality would belong. Rather, it is a bottomless hole, a black sun that would make us blind. Perhaps we should see in it that "somber mirror," symbol of an expectation full of hope, of which the Talmud speaks. Or else it is the "shadow cast by things," or by objects one on top of another and in endless movement, that makes us think of the construction *en abyme* so dear to painters of the Middle Ages and that always reveals new things to explore. But at the same time, the image, unlike the mechanism of reason, well expresses the profound organicity of everything, what I have called "holism." This explains why it is both a factor of disaggregation (that of mechanism and rationalism proper to modernity) and a factor of aggregation (around it one gathers and communes).

"Somber mirror" or construction *en abyme,* the image is, in this sense, a concentrate of the world. I have often suggested that time and history are being spatialized. An eternal instant, in a flash of lightning, expresses the cosmos in its entirety. It is just this that engenders fascination, the impassivity at issue here. Not an apathy in the trivial sense of the term, but an "impassive passion," a sort of aesthetic contemplation in which the *principium individuationis* is abolished. It is the attitude of a monk who in his solitude, by this contemplative meditation, is united with the Church as a whole. It is also, according to Nietzsche, the property of aesthetic sensibility, and finally, as I have already explained (in *The Shadow of Dionysus*), that which characterizes the orgy, that shared passion that is not projected outward (whence its impassivity) but instead is lived intensely with others. As Baudrillard says about photography, "An image has to have that quality, that of a universe from which the subject has retired," with the very texture of the object's details signifying that "interruption of the subject"[42]—a judicious phrase that stresses the loss of the subject in a universal matrix. I would add for my part that it is this matrix, crucible of indistinction, that comforts being-togetherness and is the condition of possibility of communion.

From image-liberation to image-communion, passing through image-fascination—there is only one step, or a single gradation, which is that of intensity. As a light in the night indiscriminately attracts insects that come, at the risk of their lives, to attach themselves to it, so in the same way the image, in its intensity, favors aggregation and secretes viscosity. And of course this too at the risk of death, the "little death" of the sexual act, the loss of the individual in a vaster ensemble, but a death that is the guarantee of life: of love, of the community, life that, in the long term, rebounds in its turn on the person who has no fear of being lost. We remember Novalis's fine remark that "the exterior is an interior raised to the power of mystery." Here is yet another paradox enabling us to think, if one takes literally the terms employed, that this "mystery" unites the initiated who congregate around it. Thus the transfiguration of the interior into exterior, far from signifying decadence or a loss of all values, may valorize communion for those who know. The "glorious body" of Christian mysteries is a knowing body, and personally I would say a "sensitive reason," and the exterior, another way of naming the image, is also a vector of knowledge, even if that knowledge is the property of mystery, meaning that it is shared only by some people.

But we should remember that the meganarratives, the grand systems, the universal truths have had their time, and henceforth it is only the micronarratives and provisional truths that one can share. These small ideologies—perhaps one could say these "small idols"—are plural and are evident only to some. But, so that this is not taken for elitism, let us remember that many are the tribes that share a multiplicity of idols and congregate around them. It is indeed the destiny of postmodernity to be tribal, particular, and particularized—things that are cause and effect of the eroticism, of the Dionysiac with which sociality is laden. Yet, before becoming something private, eroticism is above all collective, as we are reminded by many anthropological structures such as the bacchanalia, Dionysiac rites, and diverse orgies that have punctuated the course of human history. Like a golden thread, they are a structuring element and central to any life in society.

And when this eroticism becomes evident again, it allows itself to be seen. It shows itself to many, to a few. With essential nuances, this is what the works of the Marquis de Sade, Georges Bataille, and Pierre Klossowski enable us to understand. Thus, according to the latter, eroticism is above all a "pretext for dramaturgy," which means that "thought becomes body, spirit becomes flesh."[43] Thus one rediscovers the transfiguration already mentioned: the eroticism of the image makes a community, makes a tribal body, just as the latter nourishes the sensual and spectacular aspect of any image. What we have here is a destiny, since nothing and nobody escapes such a process. One may lament it, stigmatize it, or even, as is sometimes justified, stress the fact that the proliferation of images has something obscene about it—one's response does not matter. Too long contained, the image explodes, and explodes everything thought to have triumphed over it, too, whether centralist or Jacobin modes of organization—nation-states, centralized and perennial institutions—or ways of thinking that are no less "Jacobin"—in a nutshell, the grand homogeneous reference narratives developed in the last century.

In exploding, in making explode, the image changes from top to bottom the intellectual landscape to which we were accustomed; hence its devastating aspect. Nuclear, viral? Its deflagration, its contamination leave nothing untouched. In contrast to structures (organization and thought) that I have just called "Jacobin," in which the center and peripheries were very delineated, with the image everything is situated "elsewhere," off to the side, everything is *singular*. The tribe adores its idol and is constituted by it, but this idol could not be universal. In the same way, illustration, image, and example—unlike the concept—are things that are eminently singular and are always "alongside" of a central power, "off to the side" of where one is expecting it. It is, moreover, significant that in Greek the word that expresses example, paradigm, *para-deigma,* is "that which is shown alongside," just as in German *Beispiel* means "that which plays alongside."[44] One could insist at length on this "alongside," but it suffices that it reminds us of the importance and pregnant weight of the "small idol" in the constitution of societies: they are those unreal and singular things that are going to structure the real as it is thought, just as it is the "unreal" tribes that are going to constitute the real as it is lived.

It behooves us to apply a mode of analysis that allows us to escape the classic antinomy between the universal and the particular, or else to apply a mode of analysis that allows us to think of the real by starting with the unreal. The figurative approach may be a fruitful aid in this. The figure allows meaning to be made, and meaning to be given, not as a distant purpose or a goal to be attained, but as what I communicate or what I share with others. "The figure is what looks at us, what looks at me."[45] Gilbert Durand's phrase summarizes my thesis well: the figure is particular and it induces, by that fact, a specific enthusiasm, an ecstatic enthusiasm, or an emotional intensity that will act profoundly on social life. It is such an enthusiasm that was at the origin of the revolutions of times past, and it is quite possible that it may also be at the origin of the painful gestation, through which we are living now, of the sociality yet to come.

III. THE COMMUNITAR-
IAN IDEAL

Because one must bravely believe that what is, is.
  Vincent van Gogh

IN CONCLUSION, EVEN IF THIS seems rather tiring, let us recall that the profusion of images and the accent placed on
style signal a return to "community." For my part, in opposition to those who continue to analyze our societies in terms of
individualism and disenchantment, I have already shown that
what seems to be on the agenda involves instead a sort of tribalism, taking as its counterpart a veritable reenchantment of
the world. Starting from what is visible and immanent, there
is something that results in the invisible, in the transcendent.
It happens that in postmodern societies, that force of union,
that "manna" is quotidian, is lived here and now, and finds its
expression in an *immanent transcendence,* tending toward a
highly hedonistic color. Thus it is no longer the individual,
isolated in the fortress of his or her reason, who prevails, but
rather the tribal ensemble communing around an ensemble of
images that it consumes with voracity.

One could compare the link between the image and the community with the relation that Freud established between what he called the "composite person" and the dream: one can create a 'composite person,' serving as condensation in the dream, and in yet another way, by uniting in a single dream-image the traits of two or several people.[1] By using such a remark in a metaphoric way, and by enlarging its application, I would say that the growing share of oneiric activity in social life comes to create a "collective person," of which each individual is just a minuscule element. The dreams that one projects onto the film star of the moment, onto the celebrated sports star or the winning team, the mechanism of magic participation that makes me quiver at the mundane smile of the television anchorperson, the diverse adherences to religious or intellectual gurus—in short (if one grants this term its fullest sense), the *attraction* exercised by fashion—all this ends up creating an emotional ambience whose vibrations can be detected on the surface of things, an ambience finding its expression in a growing aestheticization of existence.

To vibrate by means of common images, to enjoy, albeit in a relative manner, the world such as it is—here are the major characteristics of an ethic of the aesthetic. The latter has been able to exist during other epochs and seems to reemerge today. It involves an effervescence that recalls that of the baroque, which, while also consisting of embellishments and trimmings, no less possessed a rigorous and solid order—enabling one to speak, in this respect, of an organic order. It is indeed this which allows us to say that an ethic of the aesthetic does exist, as a cement, a social link established on the basis of what at first could be considered frivolous, among which we must count playing with form. It happens that in the pendulum swings of the history of ideas, we regularly observe, after the saturation of a group of rationalist or classical values, the resurgence of another group of values leaning toward sensuality or the baroque. Some thinkers, historians (Eugenio d'Ors) as often as sociologists (Pitirim Sorokin, Gilbert Durand), have observed and studied the fact that cultural ensembles were characterized by a specific style (in the precise sense that this term is given), but that this style was liable to be repeated, in time, according to a cyclical type of alternation.

It is indeed this that is at stake in the tragic efflorescence of form. On the one hand, one rediscovers this characteristic in the most diverse domains, and on the other hand, it repeats ancient themes to which new meanings are given. It is striking, in fact, to see that all realms of social life, even those reputedly serious, are "contaminated" by the game of forms. This has been shown for the production of ideas, for religious life, even for politics. In each of these cases, the "product" in question is only valued to the extent that it is put into form, or that it knows how to appear, or that someone is engaged in adorning it, putting it into images—in short, that someone is involved in epiphanizing its appearance. It is the same for all enterprises, which are no longer self-sufficient but need an "image" or a "culture" to be what they are. A number of monographs bring out the role and importance of putting the industrial object into form. One discovers the same thing regarding political parties and various institutions, countries, cities, and regions that are all developing "logos" and symbols presenting the specificity or characteristic trait of the institution or place in question. In each case, image advisers, communication agencies (and public relations firms) are engaged in making visible, under a determined form, the invisible force animating, or supposedly animating, the institution that has called on their services.

It also transpires that this putting into form reinvests, most of the time, archaic themes, mythic references, or images of

the "good old days." On the model of postmodernist architecture, constructing its buildings on the basis of various
"quotations," borrowed in fact from constructions in older
styles, the imaginal world that is developing today is founded
on an archetypal substratum. It repeats in a cyclical way what
one might have thought outmoded. This is what makes us
talk of wonderment and reenchantment. The imaginary, the
symbolic, the oneiric, the festive are some of the parameters
expressing, at best, such a process. These are the archaisms
that are reinvented and reused by the various means of technological development. In this sense, one may correct the cyclical perspective already mentioned; rather, it is a spiraling
movement, in which the return of the same undergoes an important change brought about by cutting-edge technology.

There is, in the simple sense of the word, a competition
(*concurrence*) between the archaic elements and technological development; close to the word's etymology, *cum-currere,*
they "run against each other." This is the particularity of
postmodernity, to fuse contraries, to make them enter into
synergy—which does not fail to give the epoch the originality
that is its own. Such a synergy no longer has anything to do
with the causal linearity that obtained in modernity, which
gave it its force. The individual history cannot henceforward
be interpreted in terms of evolution, any more than general
history can. The royal march of Progress is over. Similarly,
Western ethnocentrism no longer applies. Cultures interpene-
trate each other, and their different temporalities contaminate
ways of being and thinking. To put it in even more clear-cut
terms, a history assured of itself gives way to a pluralist and
diversified mythology. Such a change is both cause and effect
of the resurgence of form.

In fact, form puts the stress on space and its various modulations: the body, the territory, the community, the language,

religiosity, localism. Here one might refer to what Gilbert Durand calls the "theory of recital": human life is no longer inscribed in a simple causal chain; it is made up of events embedded in a collective memory whose importance can no longer be denied—it is "re-cited." Thus one discovers the "situationism" I have spoken of, made up of eternal instants, reusing archetypal mythic figures with the aid of technological development. The "recital" is recognition, recitation, redundancy—all the things we find in diverse images, in sartorial fashion, in religious and philosophical syncretism, in architectural constructions, in figurative painting—in short, in an Orientalization of the Western world that is being pumped through the whole of social life. Of course, we should understand these "mythic Orients" in a metaphoric way. They do not come from a particular place, but rather comprise a patchwork elaborated from, say, a Hindu philosophical fragment, a Zen spiritual posture, an African piece of clothing, a South American culinary practice, a use of some "alternative" medicine—the whole forming a syncretism giving its tone to the mood of the times.

One could endlessly multiply such combinations. All are made from diverse quotations that come to be tightly organized with each other and circumscribe a new Spirit of the age whose consequences for the different ways of being-togetherness forming society are incalculable. I have suggested in what way this might make us think of baroque organicism, with the "barbarous" aspect that it unfailingly possesses. Whatever it is, the focus on such a putting into form, on such a shaping allows us to recognize very quickly the elements and general ambience resulting from their composition, which are proper to postmodernity.

I have already indicated the hermeneutic interest of such a style. Very rapidly we can signal a few similar analyses, such as d'Ors's theory of "eons." He designates the "stylistic entities" characterizing creation at a given moment: baroque or classical, for example. The same is true of the sociologist Sorokin and his theory of cyclical cultural models: there are homologous ensembles that one finds in philosophy and in literature as well as in works of culture properly speaking. And the same is true of Oswald Spengler, who stressed the "contemporaneities" beyond the artificial divisions of history. Finally, it is striking to note that the "hard sciences" do not escape such a process. Without discussing Thomas Kuhn, who well demonstrated the importance of "paradigms" in scientific research, we could also mention Gerald Holton, who in *The Scientific Imagination* pinpointed the *themata* organizing the semantic field of researchers. This goes right up to modern biology, since C. H. Waddington and Rupert Sheldrake have shown that there exist "chreodes" (necessary pathways, from *chre* ["one must"] and *odos* ["path"]) and "causative" forms in the genesis of the living or the vegetal.

Gilbert Durand, in giving an overview of all these approaches, himself uses the notion of "semantic basin," allowing us to understand the "flowing," the confluences creating the Spirit of the time, the denomination by which the latter will impose itself, its institutionalization ("the adjustment of the river banks") and its final exhaustion.[2] Such a metaphor is instructive and well takes account, at least in its initial phase of "flowing" confluences, of all the small things, the different phenomena that, by successive accumulations, are on the way to constituting the prevalence of form. From such a perspective, one well sees that it is all the more important, from a hermeneutic viewpoint, to engage in the analysis of phenomena considered frivolous by the sociological "establishment," such as bodybuilding, stylistic design, different forms of advertising, uniforms of clothing, the care of the body, the multiplication of magazines dealing with health, fashion, homes, and food, the development of parallel medicines or syncretic cults—without forgetting the New Age vogue. All these things—and the list is not complete—no longer concern just a few marginal groups, more or less intellectual or bohemian, but instead contaminate the social ensemble, bit by bit.

Nothing and nobody are immune. The influence of these phenomena is variable, modulated according to classes of age, financial resources, and professional occupations, but one can no longer avoid them—all the more so since they benefit from the support of the various media, television in particular, that merely respond, in magnifying its effects, to an expectation more or less diffused in the body social. Like a snowdrift that grows under the effect of the wind, collective sensibility, focusing on the ambient corporeality, grows in scope. Some of its elements, quite evidently, quickly become obsolete. Many are the rivulets that become exhausted when they have just started flowing, but by a kind of internal necessity, others take on force and vigor. And it is this continuous movement that is significant. In a stubborn way, the play of forms and the efflorescence of appearance are on the way to constituting a new social "skin," and it is under the protection of this integument that the body social develops.

For we are dealing with the *body* social. I have often insisted on the paradox that the exacerbation of the body proper (corporeality, fashion, appearance) ends up in its opposite and is exhausted in a collective body. Such a phenomenon should incite us to look with new eyes at the strange daily rituals that punctuate life in society, at all the tribal gatherings, the various furtive effervescences and other urban crowd situations, in which the colorful display of forms plays a crucial role. If one measures all this by the standards of modern rationalism, if one judges it as a function of utilitarianism or of content, one risks seeing only frivolity or a pure "phenomenism" of no consequence. If one seeks its meaning in the far-off or in some program, one will see in it only crazy and derisory attitudes. In this respect, one need merely think of the ethnocentrism that judged "primitive" cultures by Western criteria. Similarly, concerning the postmodern phenomena, in that frame of mind the focus on adornment and appearance is going to seem devilishly barbarous. In fact, even if only in a hypothetical way, one must appreciate the logic of form for itself and see in what way it is "forming," in what way it "makes society." It is such a Copernican revolution in the analysis of social phenomena that alone can allow us to understand the sociality, youthful in particular, that is being sketched with experimentation and hesitation at the century's close.

In contrast to a scholarly, journalistic, or political "opinion" that sees in individualism the mark of the era—which, like all conventional thought, is not up for debate—for a long time I have paid attention to the curious tribalism that tends to develop in our societies. And to develop for better or worse: the resurgence of ethnic consciousness, various religious fanaticisms, intellectual or political clans, various pressure groups and corporatisms, charitable associations, new forms of solidarity—current trends seem to corroborate this hypothesis. In this respect, we might speak of the saturation of a subjectivity of the subject, and of the consequent exhaustion of a political order constructed on such a subjectivity: that of a social contract, national as much as international. This does not mean that an objective and rational vision of the world is going to dominate. Quite the contrary: we are witnessing the birth of a veritable mass subjectivity, resting on affective contagion, on the sharing of sentiments, and on participation in common emotions. There is fanaticism in the air.

When one observes the development of human history, one

realizes that we regularly witness the resurgence of such a mass subjectivity. Various uprisings, revolts, revolutions, and other apocalypses fully demonstrate that effective contagion is far from being a new thing.[3] In those cases, the emotionalism of the being-togetherness takes the upper hand and throws all established institutions and structures into a whirl.This is manifested in various ways; virulent and brutal in revolt and revolutions, such a contagion may equally be experienced in a minor key by taking refuge in the mundane, the guarded popular attitude, and interior exile. These are evident in the disaffection regarding the political in particular and civil life in general. For my part, I consider that nowadays the play of forms, the focus on presentness, corporeality, and the sense of immanence and hedonism that all this activates are the most evident manifestations of such a revolt, or else are the particular expression of what I have called mass subjectivity. The latter is found in shared enjoyment and happiness, sometimes even in collective cruelty, a new ethic, specifically a link that is aided and abetted by the sharing of affect.

But affects, unlike pure intellectuality, have need of passage into action here and now; they must appear, show themselves, take form. One sees in what way this is far from being negligible: this is how the invisible grace of being-togetherness is visualized. Religion was not mistaken about this; through its liturgy and various rituals punctuating the ecclesiastical computation, it has always stressed the need for exteriorizing faith. And without a putting into form, this indeed remains incomplete. It finds its fulfillment only in regular and festive gatherings, weekly or daily, that make the Church into a veritable mystical body; or rather, to take up the psalmist expression, thanks to rituals, in the image of the celestial city, "everything together makes a body." Such a position, common to all religions, plays a major role in Christian theory and practice, and this as much in its orthodox theology as in a number of mystical elaborations.

Without being able to develop this point here in a relevant way, I nevertheless note that for Thomism, the "official" philosophy of Catholicism, the *Forma Ecclesia* is the very essence of the Church. This is a matter not of a vain paradox but rather of a perspective that underlines the tight connection between the essence of the ecclesial body and its expression, its form. There can be no being without appearing. As I have suggested earlier, this key concept of dogma finds its concretization in a pragmatics that is the life of the parish or community, in which the faithful live and perfect their faith. To take but one example from mysticism, I refer to a study by Père de Lubac of Friedrich Oetinger (1702–82). Recalling, in passing, the latter's influence on philosophers as diverse as Hegel, Hölderlin, and Schelling—and, we might add, therefore on a number of thinkers who during modernity were inspired by them—Henri de Lubac underlines that for the pietist Oetinger "the being of God is in the *manifestitatio sui.*" One finds this again, in echo, with Hegel, for whom "the definition of the spirit is [. . .] the manifestation [. . .]. Its definition and its content are this very manifestation." Thus, using a term created by Oetinger, he stresses the interest of "phenomenology," which, as its etymology tells us, puts the focus on what gives itself to be seen,[4] it being understood that what gives itself to be seen also refers to what gives itself to be lived. There is in the phenomenological perspective the source of the communitarian ideal. To put it another way, it is by communing together in the visible forms of the divine that one gives birth to and nurtures the community.

It transpires that nowadays this communitarian ideal is not, or no longer, lived only in churches, of whatever kind they may be. And it is no longer expressed in that profane form of religion that is politics, but is discovered, diffusely, in the whole of social life. In it, religion has become religiosity, and like the latter, the former requires forms by which and through which it is going to be expressed. This may seem irritating, but these indeed include the cult of the body, the "care for the self," alternative medicine, macrobiotic food, ecology, and dress styles that circumscribe the orbit of both religiosity and of the communitarianism that serves as its support. And one could endlessly extend the list of these phenomena that are both cause and effect of what, in a humorous way, we could call the "transcendental cosmetology" characteristic of the age. By that I mean to suggest that the form, in all its meanings, from the most banal and quotidian to the most sophisticated epistemology, is the very thing that is going to constitute the ethos, the sacred, the encompassing ambience of postmodernity.

Even if this may appear paradoxical, I will not hesitate to say that by means of form, contemporary humanism is expressed at its best. I mean by this a sensitivity to the general quality of what is human, or else, to use Montaigne's expression, that which deals with "the entire form of the human condition." Indeed, there is humanism at work when—breaking down national, partisan, and ideological barriers—a way of dressing, a kind of rock music, a pop tune, an ecological connivance, a similitude in bodily posture, or even a hairstyle serves as a sign of recognition and fosters the sentiment that one is "on equal footing" with the other. Frontiers of whatever kind become blurred, and it is human nature that is valorized instead. As we know, advertising can be considered in many respects as the mythology of the moment. To take only one example among many, one can see in the advertising variations of the Benetton stylistic—"united colors"—the mark of this humanism borne by form and lived through it. Races, countries, and skin colors have little importance from the moment that communion is established thanks to a specific image, style, or way of being.

I am forcing the issue, by way of caricature, but thereby I am suggesting a general tendency that nothing will arrest. Certainly there could be delays or else, to borrow an expression from the philosopher Ernst Bloch, "noncontemporaneities"; that is to say, there still could exist, in remnant form, attitudes, phenomena, or ways of being and thinking that still belong to modernity. This is particularly perceptible in the nationalist tensions, racist fevers, or other manifestations of intolerance whose sound and fury still resonate frequently in our societies. But this is not what is essential. As painful as are its effects, remember that dogmatism is much more an index of weakness than of strength. Above all, these "noncontemporaneities" should not make us forget the undertow wave that is the product of the conjunction between, on the one hand, a multiplicity of communities, and on the other, the spread to mass production, the massification of these same communities.

These are communities and masses that both, to different degrees, only exist by sharing images, styles, and forms that are their own. A problem remains that is far from negligible: How are these tribes and masses going to accommodate each other? How will their respective idols tolerate each other, or will they reach a compromise? In this respect we are living through a crucial moment, since the contractual model, that of a conceptual adjustment between rationally defined individuals and groups, that of intellectual negotiation, is totally saturated, but no other alternative model has yet appeared to replace it; hence the cruelty, violence, irrationalism, and even barbarism that currently seem to prevail in the clash of images, myths, or other forms of life. The emotional and affective have not found their equilibrium, are far from being at

rest. Today we can see the foreshadowing of such an equilibrium. One might even say that, like the infant who taps,
knocks, or breaks a precious object for lack of knowing how
otherwise to express his feelings, so barbarism, asserted or latent, is just a maladroit attempt to attain a harmony that it
profoundly desires and that it no longer finds in an order of
things in which it no longer recognizes itself. Let us not forget
that order is born of chaos; any birth takes place in pain.

If it is quite difficult to foresee with any certainty what this
new equilibrium will be, if one must for the moment be content
with suggesting general tendencies, one may stress its secrecy,
to quote Ernst Jünger, the fact that "suffering itself creates the
superior forces of the cure."[5] The latter might be found in a
sort of coenesthesia that, on the model of what happens in the
individual body, knows how to ally order and disorder, function and dysfunction, the static and the dynamic. It could be
the same for the body social in its ensemble. A possible sce-
nario is no longer the confrontation of ideals upheld by different nations, confrontations that inevitably lead to war with its
cortege of miseries and atrocities, but rather the conflict of images representing the diverse tribes that are their bearers, along
with what this conflict possesses of the ludic, or at the very
least, of the less bloody. Now living through a transition period, we are witnessing a war of images that, "noncontempo-
raneously," are taken for ideals (hence the various struggles in
the countries of the former Soviet empire), with the atrocities
of which we know, atrocities all the more severe in that this
war of images is "managed" by an intelligentsia—politicians,
intellectuals, technobureaucrats—who were formed within
the logic of ideas. But one can imagine that in time the confrontation of images, styles, and forms of life may enter into a logic
that is proper to it, and it may suddenly lose the sanguinary aspect that currently still belongs to it.

Such a utopia—since this is what we are talking about—is not simply an inconsequential chimera, but may be compared to the imaginings of Charles Fourier, who saw in the "war of small pies" a gentler way of experiencing human aggressiveness, or else a strategy for purging it from the body social. Fourier's metaphor is also instructive. To confront the other by offering him, in the form of a challenge, the "small pie" of one's own making may be the symbol of a return to the mundane, a recentering on what is close at hand. Now in the framework of proximity, the other, even if an enemy, is a concrete being, which drains away the murderous paranoia that invariably becomes exacerbated when that other is distant, and especially when his image is troubled by the veil of an ideal or an idea that renders him strange and potentially dangerous.

This does not mean that violence will no longer occur, since it is too constitutive of the human and social structure, but that via the war of images it may become ritualized and hence experienced at less cost or, as in ancient tournaments, only "to the first blood drawn." This is a conflictual harmony that one could calculate, a new equilibrium founded on the play of forms, a way of confronting each other via interposed images, which relativizes conflict all the more, or at the very least renders it bearable, more assimilable by the body social. Many are the clues that show that contemporary sensibility, of youth in particular, is oriented in this direction. In not recognizing itself any more in a specific ideology, in no longer believing in the dogmatism of systems forged during modernity, and in suddenly relativizing the institutions that issued from it (whether communist, socialist, or liberal), postmodern sensibility is on the way to neutralizing the polemic-generating strongholds from which modern wars were propagated. At the national level, the different modulations of the class struggle have had their day; internationally, we see clearly that the stakes can no longer be reduced to those theorized by classical geopolitics: ideological hegemony or territorial expansion. Even if the latter continue, as remnants, to exercise an effect, other problems are appearing: the environment, economic war, and cultural, religious, and ethnic conflicts—struggles for the mastery and dissemination of images.

All this has nothing more to do with what presided over the birth of the nation-state, founded on an idea or an ideal, and which must undergo their destiny: that of saturation. On the other hand, in their place surge up the country *(patrie)*, locality, community, which rest instead on a shared "form," a real and proximate image. The shock wave produced by the ideas of the French Revolution of 1789 and by those of the Enlightenment, which engendered the projects of the social contract, the democratic ideal, and the nation-state is a shock wave that is now waning. In making use of a notion (and poetic image) offered by Hölderlin in *Hyperion,* we might say that all this gives way to the "feeling for nation," designating everything that deals with the territory people share, the uses and customs issuing from it, the emotions and sentiments people experience together, the images and myths constitutive of daily life—in short, everything that both gives roots and allows a balanced growth, a link between the static and the dynamic. Modern nationalism *(national)* giving way to the postmodern feeling for nation *(nationel)*—this is not a simple wordplay.

Like a tiny iota that can change the meaning of a word, the replacement of a letter allows us to grasp the incredible upheaval that is at work these days: specifically, the slippage from a democratic, theoretical, conceptual, and distant ideal toward a communitarian ideal, that of an image, a style, a form, lived in common in the framework of the quotidian. The sociality that is being sketched on the basis of such premises has something unprecedented about it, even something disturbing, which leaves social engineering or sociometrics speechless, prisoners of habitual commonplaces and ortho- dox categories. But the groundswell that this sociality pro- pels, the intellectual challenge it throws down, is all the more exhilarating for a piloting way of thinking that does not fear turbulence and the high seas.

NOTES

PREFACE

1. Madeleine Grawitz, *Michel Bakounine* (Paris: Plon, 1990), p. 381.
2. I refer to my earlier books: *La Connaissance Ordinaire* (Paris, Méridiens-Klincksieck, 1985), the chapter on essayism, and *La Transfiguration du Politique* (Paris: Grasset, 1992), the chapter on social rhythm.
3. See R. Bastide, *Anatomie d'André Gide* (Paris: PUF, 1972), p. 21.
4. Walter Benjamin, *Le Livre des Passages* (Paris: Cerf, 1990), p. 476. On daily cynicism, see Michel Onfray, *Cynismes* (Paris: Livre de Poche, 1990), p. 54. I am indebted to Gerhard Höhn for having drawn my attention to the *Kommunitarismus-Debatte*, as well as Axel Honneth, ed., *Kommunitarismus: Eine Debatte über die moralischen Grundlagen moderner Gesellschaften* (Frankfurt and New York, 1992); Michael Walzer, "The Communitarian Critic of Liberalism," *Political Theory*, 18, no. 1 (1990); Christel Zahlmann, ed., *Kommunitarismus in der Diskussion* (Berlin: Rotbuch Verlag, 1992); Charles Taylor, *Philosophical Papers*, vol. 1, *Human Agency and Language*; vol. 2, *Philosophy and the Human Sciences* (Cambridge: Cambridge University Press, 1985); and Robert N. Bellah, *Habits of the Heart: Individualism and Commitment in American Life* (Berkeley: University of California Press, 1985).

I. TREATISE ON STYLE

1. On the theme of nostalgia, here I argue against an article, otherwise nuanced, well researched, and very interesting, by C. Bayard, "Epistemologie du Corps et Postmodernité: De l'Apocalpyse de Baudrillard à l'*Einfühlung* de Maffesoli," *Sociologie et Sociétés*, 24, no. 1 (1992).
2. See J. Marx, "L'Idée de palingénésie chez Joseph de Maistre," in *Revue des Etudes Maistriennes*, no. 5–6: *Illuminisme et Franc-Maçonnerie* (Paris: Les Belles Lettres, 1980), p. 113 ff. On the theme of attraction, see Patrick Tacussel, *L'Attraction Sociale* (Paris: Méridiens-Klincksieck, 1986). I also refer to Francisco Alberoni, *Génésis* (Paris: Ramsay, 1992).
3. Ernst Jünger, *Graffiti: Frontalières* (Paris: Bourgois, 1977), p. 25. On overlapping, see M. Shapiro, *Style, Artiste et Société* (Paris: Gallimard, 1982), pp. 38, 50. On examples from the history of art, see Heinrich Wölfflin, *Renaissance and Baroque*, trans. Kathrin Simon, intro. Peter Murray (Ithaca: Cornell University Press, 1966), p. 93; and John Ruskin, *The Stones of Venice*, ed. Jan Morris (Boston: Little Brown, 1981).
4. Shapiro, *Style, Artiste et Société*, pp. 88–89.
5. I use the word *unity* for the sake of ease. In fact, if I were faithful to my previ-

ous studies, I would here have to speak of *unicity* since the latter is not closed but, rather, assures a "dotted" coherence.

6. See *Les Cyniques Grecs,* introduction and notes by L. Paquet (Paris: Livre de Poche), p. 33. On the general idea of style as "society of an epoch," see Jean-Marie Guyau, *L'Art du Point de Vue Sociologique* (Paris: F. Alcan, 1920), p. 338.

7. Shapiro, *Style, Artiste et Société,* p. 36.

8. On the synthetic aspect of culture, see Raul Gardini, *L'Esprit de la Liturgie* (Paris: Plon, 1960), p. 37. On the expression of Saint Augustine, see the analysis by Eugenio d'Ors, *Du Baroque* (Paris: Gallimard, 1935), p. 109.

9. Hans Robert Jauss, *Toward an Aesthetic of Reception,* trans. Timothy Bahti, intro. Paul de Man (Minneapolis: University of Minnesota Press, 1982). On style as "general conception of life," see V. L. Tapié, *Baroque et Classicisme* (Paris: Le Seuil, 1980), pp. 64–65. On the "culture of sentiment," see my book *La Transfiguration du Politique* (Paris: Grasset, 1992).

10. Heinrich Wölfflin, *Principles of Art History: The Problem of the Development of Style in Later Art,* trans. M. D. Hottinger (New York: Dover Press, 1950), p. 6. On style as language, see Shapiro, *Style, Artiste et Société,* p. 43. As for ritual, see Claude Rivière and Jean Cazeneuve, *Sociologie du Rite* (Paris: PUF, 1971).

11. Emile M. Cioran, *Anathemas and Admirations,* trans. Richard Howard (New York: Arcade, 1991), p. 95. On the "common base," see Julien Gracq, *Préférences,* in *Oeuvres Complètes,* vol. 1 (Paris: "Pléiade," Gallimard, 1989), pp. 864–65.

12. Oswald Spengler, *The Decline of the West* (New York: A. A. Knopf, 1926), p. 108. On the leitmotiv and analysis of recurrent themes in Gide, see R. Bastide, *Anatomie d'André Gide* (Paris: PUF, 1972), pp. 12–14.

13. Gracq, *Préférences,* p. 980. On Erasmus, see Henri de Lubac, *Pic de la Mirandole* (Paris: Aubier, 1974), p. 69.

14. Cf. Gilbert Durand, *Beaux Arts et Archétypes* (Paris: PUF, 1989), p. 187.

15. Gilbert Simondon, *L'Individuation Psychique et Collective* (Paris: Aubier, 1989), pp. 24–25.

16. Quoted by Angela Livingstone, *Salomé: Her Life and Work* (New York: M. Bell Ltd., 1984), p. 141. See also the analysis by Hermann Broch, *Création Littéraire et Connaissance* (Paris: Gallimard, 1966), p. 148.

17. Theodor Adorno, *Notes to Literature,* vol. 1, ed. Rolf Tiedeman, trans. Sherry Weber Nicholsen (New York: Columbia University Press, 1991), p. 223.

18. Mikhail Bakunin, *Oeuvres Complètes,* vol. 7, ed. S. Lebovici (Paris), p. 278, quoted by Grawitz, *Michel Bakounine,* p. 393. On romanticism, see Ernst Benz, *Mystical Sources of German Romantic Philosophy,* trans. Blair R. Reynolds and Eunice M. Paul (Alison Park, Pa.: Pickwick Publications, 1983), p. 58.

19. Michel Foucault, *The Care of the Self,* trans. Robert Hurley (New York: Pantheon Books, 1986), pp. 238–39. On attraction, see Patrick Tacussel, *L'Attraction Sociale.* On fusion, I refer to my books *The Shadow of Dionysus,* trans. Cindy Linse and Mary Kristina Palmquist (Albany: State University of New York Press, 1993), and *Le Temps des Tribus* (Paris: Livre de Poche, 1991).

20. Broch, *Création Littéraire et Connaissance,* p. 104. On historical style, see Fritz Stern, *The Politics of Cultural Despair: A Study in the Use of German Ideology* (Berkeley: University of California Press, 1961).

21. Gilbert Durand, "La Beauté comme Présence Paraclétique," in *Eranos*

Jahrbuch (Frankfurt: Insel Verlag, 1984), p. 129. See also P. Sorokin, *Social and Cultural Dynamics* (Boston: Porter Sargent, 1957).

22. Adorno, *Notes to Literature*, p. 219. On the autonomy of forms, see William M. Johnston, *Vienna, Vienna: The Golden Age 1815–1914* (New York: C. N. Potter, 1981).

23. D'Ors, *Du Baroque*, p. 91. On the baroque as a "lifestyle," see R. Bastide, *Images du Nordeste Mystique en Noir et Blanc* (Pandora, 1978), p. 35.

24. D'Ors, *Du Baroque*, p. 29. See also Wölfflin, *Principles of Art History*, p. 21; Shapiro, *Style, Artiste et Société*, p. 51; and D. Fernandez, *Le Radeau de la Gorgone* (Paris: Grasset, 1988), p. 361.

25. Broch, *Création Littéraire et Connaissance*, p. 188. I refer here to my books *La Conquête du Présent* (Paris: PUF, 1979), and *La Connaissance Ordinaire*.

26. Georg Simmel, "Les Grandes Villes et la Vie de l'Esprit," in *Cahiers de l'Herne*, 1983, *Les Symboles du Lieu*, p. 142. See also Shapiro, *Style, Artiste et Société*, p. 71.

27. Here I rely on the excellent analysis by M. Charrière-Jacquin, "Autour de la Notion Musilienne de *Gleichnis*," *Critique de l'Ornement de Vienne à la Postmodernité*, ed. Michel Collomb and Gerard Raulet (Paris: Méridiens-Klincksieck, 1992), pp. 48–50. In a more general fashion, see Jacques L. Rider, *Modernity and Crises of Identity: Culture and Society in Fin-de-siècle Vienna* (Cambridge, Eng.: Polity Press, 1993). On analogy, I refer to the chapter I devoted to it in *La Connaissance Ordinaire*.

28. Gianni Vattimo, *End of Modernity: Nihilism and Hermeneutics in Postmodern Culture*, trans. Jon R. Snyder (Cambridge, Eng.: Polity Press and Blackwell, 1988).

29. Foucault, *Care of the Self*, p. 35.

30. Michel Foucault, *The Use of Pleasures*, trans. Robert Hurley (New York: Pantheon, 1985), p. 5.

31. Maurizio Ferraris, *Ermeneutica di Proust* (Milano: Ed. Guerini, 1987), p. 9.

32. See Philippe Pons, *D'Edo à Tokyo: Memoires et Modernités* (Paris: Gallimard, 1988), pp. 153, 282.

33. Guyau, *L'Art du Point de Vue Sociologique*, p. 19. On linkage, see Marcel Bolle de Bal, *La Tentation Communautaire* (Brussels: 1984), and René Schérer, *L'Ame Atomique, pour une Esthétique d'ère Nucléaire* (Paris: Albin Michel, 1986), p. 178.

34. Francis Jacques, *Difference and Subjectivity: Dialogue and Personal Identity*, trans. Andrew Rothwell (New Haven: Yale University Press, 1991), p. xxviii. On copresence, see Antony Giddens, *The Constitution of Society: Outline of the Theory of Structuralism* (Berkeley: University of California Press, 1984). On identification, I refer to my book *Aux Creux des Apparences* (Paris: Livre de Poche, 1993).

35. Jacques, *Difference and Subjectivity*, p. xxi.

36. Ibid., p. xxv.

37. Ibid., p. 7.

38. Ibid., p. 7. See also Abraham Moles, *Théorie de l'Information et Perception Esthétique* (1972), p. 104.

39. Emile Durkheim, *Elementary Forms of Religious Life*, trans. Joseph Ward Swain (New York: Free Press, 1965).

40. Umberto Eco, *La Guerre du Faux* (Paris: Livre de Poche, 1985), p. 197. On

the *telenovelas,* see I. Pennacchioni, "The Reception of Popular Television in Northeast Brazil," in *Sociétiés,* no. 7 (1986).

II. THE IMAGINAL WORLD

1. Quoted in Julien Benda, *Essai d'un Discours Cohérent sur les Rapports de Dieu et du Monde* (Paris: 1931), p. 43.
2. Jacques L. Rider, *Le Cas Otto Weininger* (Paris: 1982), p. 202.
3. See Rider, *Modernity and Crises of Identity,* p. 49.
4. Gilbert Durand, *Les Structures Anthropologiques de l'Imaginaire* (Paris: Seuil, 1965), p. 178. On the "iconic," see the suggestive study by A. Arnaud, *Pierre Klossowski* (Paris: Seuil, 1990), par ex. 157.
5. Miguel de Unamuno, *Journal Intime* (Paris: 1990), p. 45; *The Private World: Selections from Diario Intimo,* trans. Anthony Kerrigan, Allen Lacy, and Martin Nozick (Princeton: Princeton University Press, 1984).
6. Jean Baudrillard, *The Transparency of Evil: Essays on Extreme Phenomena,* trans. James Benedict (New York and London: Verso, 1993), pp. 17–18.
7. Giorgio Agamben, *The Coming Community,* trans. Michael Hardt (Minneapolis: University of Minnesota Press, 1993). One should also check Guy Debord, *Society of the Spectacle* (New York: Zone Books, 1994).
8. See Y. Ishagpour, *Elias Canetti* (Paris: 1990), p. 152.
9. Serge Gruzinski, *La Guerre des Images: De "Christophe Colomb" à "Blade Runner"* (Paris: 1990), pp. 41 or 158.
10. Sigmund Freud, *Leonardo da Vinci and a Memory of His Childhood,* trans. Alan Tyson (New York: Norton, 1964), p. 19.
11. Foucault, *Care of the Self,* p. 139. See also Jacques, *Difference and Subjectivity,* p. 83.
12. See Werner Jaeger, *Paideai: The Ideals of Greek Culture,* 2 vols., trans. Gilbert Highet (Oxford: Oxford University Press, 1939–46), 1:152, 2:81.
13. Pierre Klossowski, *Le Mage du Nord* (Montpellier: 1988). This analysis of J. G. Hamann by Klossowski is cited in Arnaud, *Pierre Klossowski,* p. 138.
14. Cf. Gilbert Durand, "La Beauté comme Présence Paraclétique," p. 144.
15. Durand, *Beaux Arts et Archétypes,* p. 243; on the baroque, I also refer to my book *Aux Creux des Apparences,* p. 138.
16. On Joaquim of Floris, see the remarkable book by Henri de Lubac, *La Posterité Spirituelle de Joaquim de Flore,* 2 vols. (Paris: 1979), specifically 1:46.
17. Franco Ferrarotti, *I grattaciele non Hanno Foglie* (Rome: Laterza, 1991), p. 29.
18. Here I rely on Ishagpour's study, *Elias Canetti,* pp. 16, 32. I have developed this idea in my book *La Violence Totalitaire* (Paris: 1979), chap. 1, "Pouvoir-Puissance." On figurative sociology, I refer to Patrick Tacussel, "L'Avènement de la Sociologie" (doctoral thesis, Sorbonne, 1993).
19. Serge Moscovici, *The Invention of Society: Psychological Explanations for Social Phenomena,* trans. W. D. Halls (Cambridge, Eng.: Polity Press, 1993), p. 76. See also Franco Ferrarotti, *Faith without Dogma: The Place of Religion in Postmodern Societies* (New Brunswick, N.J.: Transaction Publishers, 1993). I have treated the problem of religiosity in my *Temps des Tribus.*

20. Durkheim, *Elementary Forms of Religious Life.*

21. Emile Durkheim, *La Science Social et l'Action* (Paris: PUF, 1970), pp. 196–97. On linkage, I refer to Bolle de Bal, *Tentation Communautaire.*

22. See Gianni Vattimo, *Ethique de l'Interprétation* (Paris: 1991), pp. 20–22.

23. Georg Simmel, *La Tragédie de la Culture* (Paris: 1988), pp. 234–35.

24. Livingstone, *Salomé.*

25. Durand, *Beaux Arts et Archetypes,* p. 144.

26. Cf. Walter Benjamin, "The Life of Students," trans. Ken Frieden, in *A Jewish Journalist at Yale* 2:1 (fall 1984), pp. 46–55.

27. See the references to Robert Grossteste or to Albertus Magnus in Georges Duby, *The Age of Cathedrals: Art and Society 980–1420,* trans. Eleanor Levieux and Barbara Thompson (Chicago: University of Chicago Press, 1981), p. 148.

28. See Moscovici, *Invention of Society,* pp. 108–10, and the references he gives to Mauss and Durkheim. See also H. Halbwachs, *La Topographie Legendaire de la Terre Sainte* (Paris: PUF, 1941), and Gérard Namer, *Mémoire et Société* (Paris: Méridiens-Klincksieck, 1987).

29. Robert Park, "The Urban Community as a Spatial Pattern and a Moral Order," in his *On Social Control and Collective Behavior* (Chicago: Phoenix Books, 1967), pp. 55–68.

30. Concerning Schleiermacher and the romantic "feeling with," see Marc Michel, *La Théologie aux Prises avec la Culture: De Schleiermacher à Tillich* (Paris: Cerf, 1982), p. 74. On Japanese examples, see Pons, *D'Edo à Tokyo,* pp. 250–52.

31. Gilles Deleuze, *The Fold: Leibniz and the Baroque,* trans. Tom Conley (Minneapolis: University of Minnesota Press, 1993), p. 115. On "formism," I refer to my book *La Connaissance Ordinaire.*

32. Arthur Schopenhauer, *World as Will and Representation,* trans. E. F. J. Payne (New York: Dover Press, 1969).

33. See Simondon, *L'Individuation Psychique et Collective,* pp. 18–20.

34. Gruzinski, *Guerre des Images,* p. 86.

35. Deleuze, *The Fold,* p. 125. On reification, see Georg Lukács, *History and Class Consciousness: Studies in Marxist Dialectics,* trans. Rodney Livingstone (Cambridge: MIT Press, 1971), and the magazine *Internationale Situationniste,* 1972. See also Jean Baudrillard, *Revenge of the Crystal: Selected Writings on the Modern Object 1968–1983,* trans. Paul Fons and Julian Pefanis (London and Concord, Mass.: Pluto Press, 1990).

36. See the studies of R. Shields and Ricardo Ferreria on shopping centers (CEAQ, Paris V). On design, see Félix Torres, *Déjà Vu: Post et Néo-modernisme, le Retour du Passé* (Paris: Ramsay, 1986), pp. 18–181.

37. Daniel Bensaïd, *Walter Benjamin: Sentinelle Messianique à la Gauche du Possible* (Paris: Plon, 1990), p. 91. For the Marx quotation, see *The Letters of Karl Marx,* trans. and ed. Saul K. Padavor (Englewood Cliffs, N.J.: Prentice-Hall, 1979), p. 282. On "copresence," see Giddens, *The Constitution of Society.*

38. P. Evdokimov, *Les Ages de la Vie Spirituelle des "Pères" du Désert à nos Jours* (Paris: 1980), p. 178.

39. Adorno, *Notes on Literature,* 2:228.

40. Vattimo, *Ethique de l'Interpretation,* p. 22.

41. Quoted by Andrea Livingstone in *Salomé,* p. 161. On transfiguration, see Raymond Abellio, *Approches de la Nouvelle Gnose* (Paris: 1981), p. 28. On music

videos, I refer to the research by N. Deville, *La Mythologie dans les Vidéoclips* (CEAQ, Paris V); and on androgyny, to the research of J. L. Juif, *L'Androgyne dans la Publicité* (CEAQ, Paris V).

42. Jean Baudrillard, *La Transparence du Mal* (Paris: 1990), p. 159. On Nietzsche, see J. Rider, *Modernity and Crisis of Identity*. Finally, see my book on the orgy, *Shadow of Dionysus*.

43. Arnaud, *Pierre Klossowski*, p. 170.

44. Agamben, *Coming Community*, p. 10.

45. Gilbert Durand, *"Mitolusimo" de Lima de Freitas* (Lisbon: 1987), p. 10. On figurative sociology, see also the doctoral thesis by Patrick Tacussel and his book, *L'Attraction Sociale*.

III. THE COMMUNITARIAN IDEAL

1. Sigmund Freud, *The Interpretation of Dreams,* trans. A. A. Brill (New York: Modern Library and Random House, 1978).

2. Cf. Durand, "Beauté comme Présence Paraclétique," pp. 128–29. See also Durand, *Beaux Arts et Archétypes,* p. 22.

3. Regarding this see the masterwork by Norman Cohn, *The Pursuit of the Millennium: Revolutionary Millenarians and Mystical Anarchists of the Middle Ages* (New York: Oxford University Press, 1970).

4. Cf. de Lubac, *Pic de la Miraudole,* pp. 248–49. On ritual, see the books of Claude Rivière.

5. Ernst Jünger, "Gardens and Streets," *Journal I, 1939–1940* (Paris: Bourgois, 1979), p. 209. On the end of the nation-state, see Ernst Jünger, "La Cabane dans la Vigne," *Journal IV, 1945–1948* (Paris: Bourgois, 1980), p. 255. Concerning humanism, one might consult Julien Benda, *La Trahison des Clercs* (Paris: Grasset, 1975), pp. 153–54.

INDEX

Compiled by Robin Jackson

MICHEL MAFFESOLI is professor of sociology at the University of Paris (I) Sorbonne. He is the author of numerous books, the most recent being *The Transfigurations of Politics* (1992).

SUSAN EMANUEL has been a producer of educational television programs for the BBC and a lecturer in film and television studies at the University of Bristol, Yale, and MIT. She has a doctorate in communications from Rennes University in France and has translated works by Pierre Bourdieu and Armand Mattelart. She lives with her family outside Boston and in Brittany.